— Tracking —
Fred Harvey's Southwest Indian Detours

Mike Butler

FONTHILL

(*A note on the photographs: Unattributed photographs were taken by the author or are from his collection. The source of all other photographs is noted in their captions.*)

Fonthill Media Inc.
www.fonthillmedia.com
office@fonthillmedia.com

First published 2024

ISBN 978-1-62545-126-2

Typeset in 10pt on 13pt Sabon
Printed and bound in England

Contents

About the Author

Since retiring as an administrative manager in the Denver Parks & Recreation Department, Mike Butler has been traveling and researching local histories in Colorado and New Mexico. He has written five books for Arcadia Publishing's *Images of America* series including *Around the Spanish Peaks; Great Sand Dunes National Park; Southern Colorado: O.T. Davis Collection; Littleton;* and *High Road to Taos*. He has also written four books for Fonthill Media's *America Through Time* series including *Tracking the Chili Line Railroad to Santa Fe; Tracking the Narrow Gauge From Chama to Durango; Tracking Rocky Mountain Railroad Club Excursions 1987–1990;* and *Getting Around in Glacier National Park.*

Introduction

New Mexico is the kind of place that will stop you in your tracks. And if you were riding the Atchison, Topeka and Santa Fe Railway's passenger train across New Mexico in the late 1920s, the tracks would lead you to stops at Raton, Las Vegas, Lamy, Albuquerque, and Gallup. At each stop a Harveycar would be waiting to take you on an "Indian Detour" across mountains, deserts, and canyons to visit exotic places like Santa Fe and Taos and see living Indian villages in adobe pueblos that were hundreds of years old. You didn't have to rough it either—at the end of each day's journey there was a comfortable Fred Harvey Hotel waiting for you with clean rooms and excellent dining. Irvin S. Cobb, an early traveler in the 1900s described this as "roughing it deluxe" in his book by that title:

> Starting out from Chicago on the Santa Fe, we had a full trainload ... we were going West to see the country and rough it—rough it on overland trains better equipped and more luxurious than any to be found in the East; rough it at ten-dollar-a-day (Fred Harvey) hotels ... There is another detail of the Harvey system that makes you wonder...right out there in the middle of nowhere, stands a hotel big enough and handsome enough for Chicago or New York, built in the Spanish style ... It is flanked by flower-beds and refreshingly green strips of lawn, with spouting fountains scattered about.[1]

Roughing it deluxe indeed.

So, the creation of the Southwest Indian Detours is perhaps best understood in the context of the development of the Fred Harvey Company in the late 1800s. Rail travel across the Southwest in the 1870s was pretty miserable for passengers. Coaches were hot, open windows allowed dust and cinders into the cars, and meals were spotty and often consisted of rancid beef and beans served at the cantinas where the train's steam engine stopped to take on water and coal. "Prior to Fred Harvey's arrival in 1876, travelers on the AT&SF were offered two types of food: barely edible and badly spoiled."[2] Fred Harvey was an English immigrant, who came to America in 1853 at the age of seventeen. Fred found work as a dishwasher at a New York restaurant and worked his way up to busboy, waiter, and line cook, learning as much as he could about the business.

On July 27, 1858, Fred Harvey became an American citizen. He eventually moved westward to St. Louis and then to St. Joseph, Missouri, working for a small regional railroad as a postal clerk and then as a passenger agent. This combination of knowledge of the restaurant business and railroading served Fred well in his future career. As a passenger agent he traveled extensively on the nation's rails, selling tickets, and eating the horrible food in train stations. Something had to be done. "Fred was certain it was possible to serve the finest cuisine imaginable along the train tracks in the middle of nowhere."[3]

Fred's opportunity came in January 1876, when he took over management of a twenty-seat lunch counter on the second floor of the Atchison, Topeka and Santa Fe (AT&SF) train station in Topeka, Kansas. Bringing in fresh food on AT&SF trains, Fred Harvey created the first of what would eventually be a network of highly successful restaurants and hotels across the Southwest. For his restaurants, he hired young women as waitresses, hoping to bring a soothing, cultured tone to the Wild West. This was quite a good opportunity for women in the Victorian Age, whose general station in life was to stay at home and be a good housewife. Becoming a "Harvey Girl" meant the excitement of traveling on an AT&SF train to restaurant employment far from home, where they would stay in company lodging and have meals and wages provided. In exchange, the Harvey Girls agreed not to get married for six months. This caveat was necessary because there were so few women in the West that men quickly sought Harvey Girls as wives.

Throughout his career, Fred Harvey worked hand in glove with the Atchison, Topeka and Santa Fe Railway.

> The two companies' identities were so closely intertwined that one scarcely knew where the Santa Fe Railway ended, and the Fred Harvey Company began. Their illustrated books, pamphlets, folios, menus, postcards, playing cards, timetables, calendars, and even matchbook covers evoke vivid images of the joys and adventure of the journey through a previously remote world. They made travel … easy, comfortable, affordable, and attractive to the masses.[4]

For Fred Harvey's restaurants and hotels, the AT&SF would provide the buildings and utilities, "as well as free transportation for all Harvey employees and supplies. Fred Harvey provided the furniture, linen, and tableware, and received all proceeds for meals sold."[5]

The symbiotic relationship between the railroad and Fred Harvey worked so well that Fred Harvey became the nation's first recognizable "chain" enterprise.

> Fred Harvey created the first national chain of restaurants, of hotels, of newsstands, and of bookstores—in fact, the first national chain of anything—in America. But unlike the chains of today, the Fred Harvey system was known for dramatically raising standards wherever it arrived … At its peak, Fred Harvey had over sixty-five restaurants and lunch counters, sixty dining cars, a dozen large hotels, all the restaurants and retail shops in five of the nation's largest railroad stations, and so many newsstands and bookshops that its prepublication orders regularly affected national best-seller lists.[6]

Right: Fred Harvey later in life. [*New Mexico History Museum exhibit*]

Below: Noted for "delicious meals." Fred Harvey Houses were located all along the Atchison, Topeka & Santa Fe Railway line to serve hungry train passengers. [*June 11, 1939, AT&SF Timetables brochure*]

Perhaps an inevitable outcome of the success of Fred Harvey's hotels and restaurants was the desire to bring even more income to the company by inducing train travelers to stay longer. This could be done by offering motor coach service from the hotels to the remote country of New Mexico and Arizona, prompting guests to stay one, two, three nights, or even longer, in a Harvey hotel. These tours would be through "Indian Country," visiting ancient ruins and adobe pueblos with native inhabitants performing ritual dances and offering handmade items for sale. Thus, were born the Indian Detours of the Southwest, offered by the Fred Harvey Company. "In a Harveycar, the entire Southwest suddenly opened up to people who were afraid to drive across one of our last frontiers by themselves."[7]

FRED HARVEY DINING STATIONS AND HOTELS

LOCATION	Seating Capacity		Number of Guest Rooms
	Lunch Room	Dining Room	
Albuquerque, New Mexico (Alvarado Hotel.	124	120	121
Ash Fork, Arizona (Escalante Hotel)	128	...	21
Bakersfield, California	47	...	...
Barstow, California (Casa del Desierto Hotel)	52	...	29
Belen, New Mexico	45	...	...
Canadian, Texas	38	* 60	...
Chicago, Illinois (Dearborn Station)	34	76	...
Clovis, New Mexico (Gran Quivira Hotel)	54	98	35
Dodge City, Kansas (El Vaquero Hotel)	101	...	41
El Paso, Texas (Union Station)	43	69	...
Gallup, New Mexico (El Navajo Hotel)	97	108	71
Grand Canyon, Arizona (El Tovar Hotel)	...	200	77
" " " (Bright Angel Lodge)	222	...	146
Houston, Texas (Union Station)	91	...	...
Hutchinson, Kansas (Bisonte Hotel)	48	110	67
Kansas City, Missouri (Union Station)	394	140	...
La Junta, Colorado (Fred Harvey Hotel)	64	76	39
Lamy, New Mexico (El Ortiz Hotel)	34	12	8
Las Vegas, New Mexico (Castaneda Hotel)	110	...	36
Los Angeles, California (Union Station)	278	...	...
Needles, California (El Garces Hotel)	116	...	26
Newton, Kansas	115	...	...
San Bernardino, California	74	...	...
Seligman, Arizona (Fred Harvey Hotel)	48	* 86	19
Slaton, Texas	46	...	...
Somerville, Texas (Fred Harvey Hotel)	50	...	20
Santa Fe, New Mexico (La Fonda Hotel)	...	350	147
Topeka, Kansas	74	...	...
Vaughn, New Mexico (Las Chaves Hotel)	42	...	10
Williams, Arizona (The Fray Marcos)	53	72	37
Winslow, Arizona (La Posada Hotel)	124	...	67

* Coffee Shop.

The station hotels are conveniently located for business and sightseeing. Rates (European Plan) for one person range from $1.50 per day up for rooms without bath and from $2.50 per day up for rooms with bath.

From Chicago, Illinois to Los Angeles, California the Fred Harvey "chain" served guests in lunchrooms, dining rooms, and hotels with great meals and clean rooms. *[June 11, 1939, AT&SF Timetables brochure*]

Above left: Fred Harvey sold books, magazines, and newspapers at train stations across the country. This was a sign from one of his bookshops. [*New Mexico History Museum exhibit*]

Above right: This sign carved by one of the drivers of the Detours, hung in the lobby of the La Fonda Hotel in Santa Fe pointing to more information for travelers. Today the sign hangs in the Detours At La Fonda Shop in the hotel lobby.

1

The Genesis of the Indian Detours

Well before the Indian Detours could begin though, the Atchison, Topeka and Santa Fe Railway had to open the way for travelers to cross the Southwest to reach Los Angeles on a transcontinental route from Chicago. AT&SF laid tracks (and then a tunnel) across Raton Pass on the border of Colorado and New Mexico in 1879, proceeding south to Raton and Las Vegas, and then west to Santa Fe. The railroad had planned to follow the old Santa Fe Trail across Kansas, Colorado, and New Mexico to the capital city of its namesake—Santa Fe. However, upon reaching the small settlement of Lamy, the railroad determined that the next eighteen miles uphill to Santa Fe would be too steep of a grade for its steam engines and trains. So, Santa Fe was bypassed, much to the consternation of its citizens. Passengers departing at Lamy had to be transported by stagecoach (and later Harveycars) up to Santa Fe. Inconvenient yes, but still providing a sense of adventure for travelers. The railroad proceeded west to Albuquerque, and then across New Mexico to Gallup and into Arizona, home of the Grand Canyon.

Since the AT&SF line was about sixty miles south of the Grand Canyon, "actual guided tours for Santa Fe Railway passengers began as wagon excursions to the Grand Canyon."[1] The railroad eventually built a spur line to the Grand Canyon in 1901, creating a boom in Southwest tourism which continues to this day. Getting passengers to the Canyon was one thing, lodging was another. AT&SF built the El Tovar Hotel right on the rim of the Canyon and opened it in 1905 with Fred Harvey as concessionaire.

When motorcars arrived on the scene, Fred Harvey's "Harveycars provided seven different tours of the Grand Canyon in 1915."[2] It was these "Harveycars," managed by the Fred Harvey Company's transportation manager at the Grand Canyon, Major R. Hunter Clarkson, which provided the seed which would germinate into Clarkson's plan for the Indian Detours in 1926. Clarkson was a decorated British military officer with logistics experience. It was his responsibility to operate a transportation network of cars and coaches, carrying tourists for the Fred Harvey Company from its El Tovar Hotel on primitive roads along the Canyon rim, seven miles west to Hermit's Rest and twenty-five miles east to Desert View.

> By 1919, the "El Tovar-Desert View Road" was still nothing to boast about ... Fred Harvey crews (kept) it passable for scenic tours ... Because of frequent breakdowns and

The AT&SF tunnel under Raton Pass was completed within a year after the initial crossing of the pass by the railroad in 1879. [*Fred Harvey booklet The Great Southwest, 1911*]

The AT&SF station in Lamy, New Mexico is still standing, and today serves Amtrak passengers departing for Santa Fe. Harveycars no longer transport passengers from Lamy to Santa Fe, but local shuttle services do.

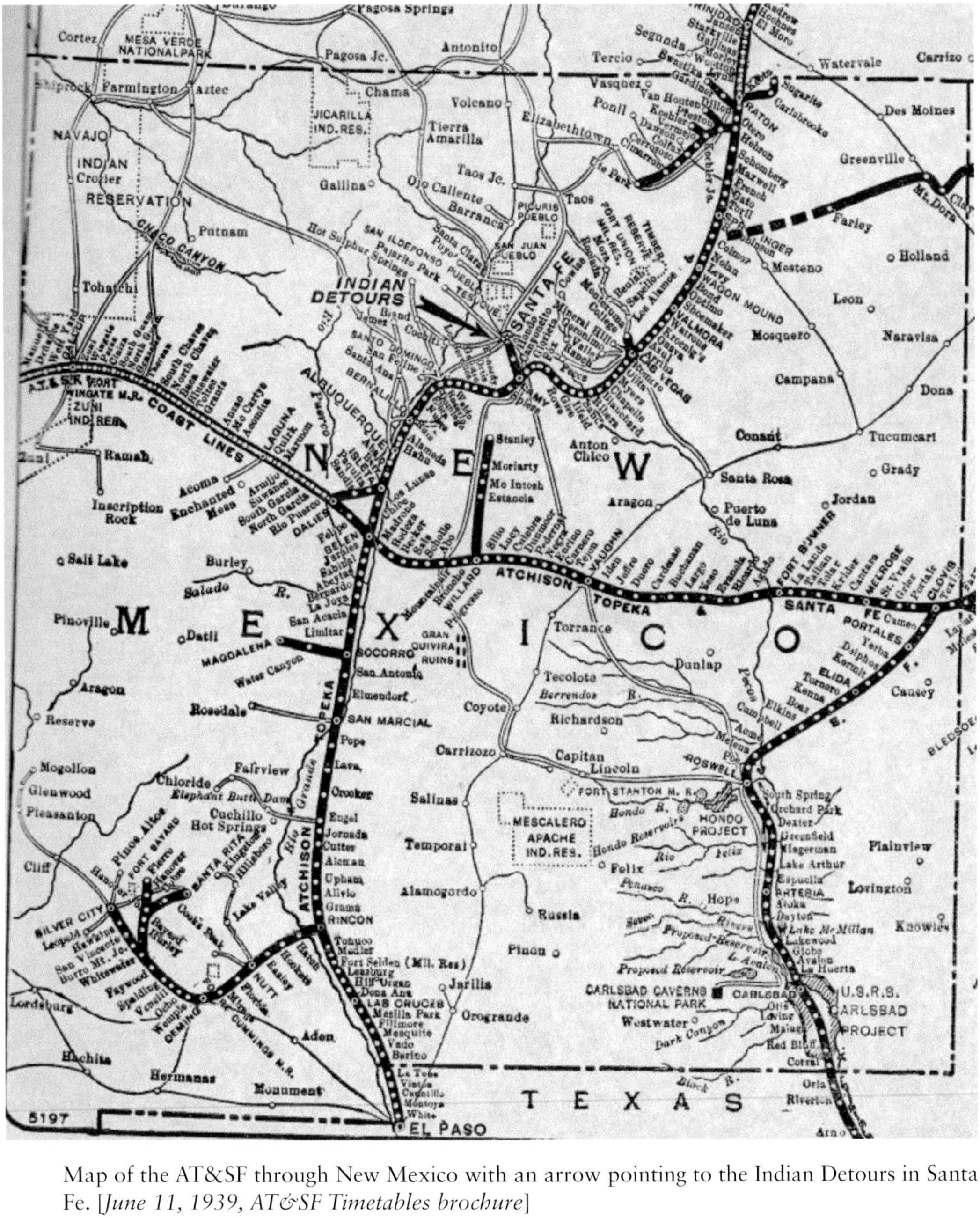

Map of the AT&SF through New Mexico with an arrow pointing to the Indian Detours in Santa Fe. [*June 11, 1939, AT&SF Timetables brochure*]

Before the AT&SF arrived at the Grand Canyon in 1901, tourists were brought in by stagecoaches such as this one racing to the rim, c. 1900. [*Photograph by Charles Pierce, PhotCLPierce 09661, Huntington Library, San Marino, California*]

Since the railroad was sixty miles from the Grand Canyon, this dinner station was set up halfway to the Canyon, c. 1900, to refresh passengers. It probably did not meet Fred Harvey standards. [*Photograph by George Thresher, PhotCL449(9), Huntington Library*]

The First AT&SF train arrives at the Grand Canyon in 1901. [*National Park Service*]

Over 50,000 visitors per year were arriving by train at the Grand Canyon by 1920. This log station was their arrival point. [*Library of Congress, HAER AZ-41-7*]

> other difficulties, drivers carried passenger pigeons to signal for help, and passengers rented linen dusters, hats, and goggles as protection from the mud and dust.[3]

Despite these difficult conditions, visitors flocked to these tours by the thousands. Clarkson "was shuttling more than fifty thousand visitors a year around the canyon with military precision."[4] Clarkson's success was duly noted in Fred Harvey corporate offices in Kansas City.

When Fred Harvey passed away in 1901, his oldest son Ford, took the reins of the business which became not the "Fred Harvey Company," but simply "Fred Harvey." His father had been so successful that Ford was loathe to call the company anything except Fred Harvey. In 1925, with the post-World War I economy booming, Ford:

> was finally convinced to make a move to Santa Fe. Hunter Clarkson, the company's ambitious head of transportation at the Grand Canyon ... convinced Ford that Fred Harvey could take the kind of bus and car tourism that had become very popular in and around the South Rim and expand it all the way across Arizona and New Mexico. He proposed a project called Indian Detours, which would basically create a new, well-advertised Native tourism corridor between the Grand Canyon and Las Vegas, New Mexico. Any site not on the rail line would be reached by a new fleet of Packard "Harveycars" and "Harveycoaches" ... and regardless of which direction the tourists were coming from, they would all end taking those tours from a home base (Santa Fe).[5]

Thus, when Clarkson approached Ford Harvey with his idea for the Indian Detours, he found a willing listener. Clarkson proposed that the Indian Detours be headquartered in Santa Fe, which was halfway between two Fred Harvey hotels—the Castañeda in Las Vegas, New Mexico, and the Alvarado in Albuquerque.

Tourists prepare to leave El Tovar Hotel at the Grand Canyon by horse-drawn coach for a trip along the South Canyon Rim, c. 1905. [*National Park Service*]

Above: The Castañeda Hotel in Las Vegas, New Mexico, was opened in 1899 and serviced by Fred Harvey. It was the departure point for the first Indian Detour in 1926. Closed in 1948, it fell into ruin, until restoration was completed by Allan Affeldt in 2019. Here, the front hotel plaza is being finished just before the grand re-opening.

Right: The luxurious Alvarado Hotel in Albuquerque, photographed here c. 1922, opened in 1902 and was operated by Fred Harvey. It closed in 1969 and was torn down in 1970. [*Library of Congress, LC-USZ62-116105*]

In Santa Fe a hotel would have to be purchased, and the AT&SF obliged by purchasing the La Fonda Hotel on the plaza in 1926. The La Fonda Hotel would serve Harvey guests with Harveycar departures both east and west, north and south. From this starting point the Indian Detours blossomed into tours all across New Mexico and Arizona. It would be Fred Harvey hotels and restaurants which would serve the "dudes" as the tourists came to be affectionately known. "Hunter Clarkson believed that Fred Harvey could corner the entire dude market."[6]

Now the planning for the Indian Detours really began in earnest. Clarkson moved from the Grand Canyon to Santa Fe to set up operations. A great deal had to be accomplished in just one year's time in order to meet the projected starting date of May 1926. Vehicles had to be ordered, purchased, and transported to Santa Fe. And just as well-trained "Harvey Girls" served delicious meals in Fred Harvey restaurants, so would well-trained women "Couriers" have to be hired and trained for the Detours as guides. Drivers would have to be hired for the cars and coaches. The La Fonda Hotel had to be spruced up to meet Harvey standards.

Clarkson set about ordering his fleet of vehicles for the Detours. He ordered coaches from the Yellow Coach Company in two different models—the X model could carry sixteen passengers, and the Y model could carry twenty-six. "The leather upholstered seats were designed to swivel so passengers could see without a lot of head turning. The coaches were made with huge plate glass windows for good visibility."[7] Clarkson also ordered nineteen buses from the White Motor Company of Cleveland. "They, too, had swivel seats, large windows and carried 13 including the Courier and Driver."[8] For automobiles, Clarkson ordered a fleet of nine 7-passenger cars from Packard which "arrived at the Santa Fe Transportation Garage on April 15, 1926."[9] The official Thunderbird logo of the Fred Harvey Company was painted on the sides of the buses and cars. Herman Schweizer, Indian arts and crafts buyer for Fred Harvey, designed the logo from an image that he had seen on Native rock art at the Abo Cliffs near Mountainair, New Mexico.

A Thunderbird pin was designed to be worn on the hat of the Couriers. Clarkson deferred to the expertise of the female Couriers for the design of the rest of the costume for the Couriers. Besides the cloche hat with the pin, colorful velveteen blouses in Navajo style were to be worn, with "squash-blossom" turquoise and silver necklaces. A silver and turquoise concha belt was to be worn around the waist. The skirt was a dark color with a large pleat for easy movement, though skirts could be replaced with pants when the women were climbing ladders at the Puye and Bandelier cliff ruins. Sturdy boots would complete the Courier outfit. The drivers looked like "Scoutmasters" with a large Stetson hat, "leather puttees ending in widely flaring khaki jodhpurs. Blousy gay plaid shirts were made even more colorful by a huge silk neckerchief ... the ends reaching to his beltline. His belt buckle was more than likely to be a heavy silver one, set with turquoise."[10]

The Couriers had to be trained to give accurate tours to the dudes, and here Clarkson had the good fortune to come across Erna Fergusson's Koshare Tours which had been operating in Santa Fe since 1921. Fergusson was a:

> personal guide to the many people who came to Santa Fe with a desire to explore beyond the city limits. Her 7-passenger air-cooled Franklin sedan ... was a familiar sight in the pueblos. She had many friends among the Indians, a friendship which allowed her unusual freedom of the pueblos and a chance to get "close" to the occupants.[11]

Harveycars and Harveycoaches leave the Castañeda Hotel for one of the first Indian Detours in 1926. Note the drivers with their Stetson hats. [*Photograph in the train station waiting room in Las Vegas*]

The thunderbird served as the official logo for Fred Harvey, and this silver thunderbird pin was worn on the hat of the Indian Detour Couriers. Note the "Harveycars" script at the bottom of the pin.

Above left: At the 2019 re-opening of the Castañeda Hotel, the roles of Harvey Courier (left) and Harvey Girl (right) were re-enacted with these costumes.

Above right: The Harveycar drivers were outfitted with Stetson hat, plaid shirt, long neckerchief, silver/turquoise belt buckle, and khaki jodhpur pants. [*New Mexico History Museum exhibit*]

In Santa Fe, Fergusson became known as the "first woman dude wrangler," and Clarkson was only too pleased to purchase her company and put her to work for Fred Harvey. Clarkson and Fergusson decided on the requirements for Couriers: the women had to be college graduates, at least twenty-five years old, with a familiarity of the Southwest and preferably able to speak Spanish because most of the Indians of the pueblos could speak Spanish. Training for the first twenty women Couriers began on April 15, 1926. Two of the Couriers had been with Koshare tours, and they helped with the training. The Couriers "were given an enormous amount of historical material to memorize, from scripts and manuals created by the Company,"[12] particularly by Erna Fergusson. When the Detours began, Fergusson led some of the tours herself and guided the dudes to the Pueblo Indian dances in New Mexico and Arizona. This led her to write her now classic book, *Dancing Gods: Indian Ceremonials of New Mexico and Arizona*, published in 1931.

The Couriers were paid \$150/month with an extra \$10/month if they were fluent in another language. They were not allowed to accept tips from the dudes. If a dude insisted on tipping a Courier, the Courier could discreetly suggest that upon returning home, the dude could mail her a "gift." All expenses away from home base were paid (by Fred Harvey)—meals, accommodations, entrance fees—and the girls were able to save enough to buy fine Indian jewelry and fatten a bank account."[13] On the tours, Couriers were encouraged to try to answer all questions from the dudes:

> but however bizarre the questions might seem to a Westerner (to this day many Easterners still think New Mexico is a foreign country), the courier and driver were supposed to maintain their composure. Major Clarkson was known to send "spy dudes" out on the trail just to test the couriers. The Detourist was an honored guest; he or she would not be insulted by an impatient Detours employee.[14]

Some Couriers were assigned "train duty" which entailed boarding the AT&SF train at either Lamy or Albuquerque and handing out Indian Detour brochures and selling Detour tickets. One Courier was usually sent to large eastern cities for three months after Christmas to promote the Detours on speaking engagements, again handing out brochures and selling tickets.

Requirements for the drivers were not as strict as for the Couriers. A college education was not required. Drivers were not expected to be tour guides answering questions. They were expected to be mechanically inclined so that they could accomplish minor vehicle repairs and change flat tires on the roads.

> Drivers were required to carry an inner tube, fan belt, spark plugs, a distributor, plus a tarp for traction and a shovel, and were supposed to know how to make minor repairs using the spare parts ... Most of the problems could be summed up in a word—flats. Tires were "iffy" and roads were primitive; the combination usually meant a tour without a tire change was an exception.[15]

The roads across the deserts of New Mexico and Arizona were largely unpaved. Rainstorms caused flash flooding in sandy arroyos which the Harveycars had to drive through. Even after waiting for the flood to pass, drivers often got stuck in the wet sand in the arroyos. Since there was no telephone or radio communication with the Transportation Garage in Santa Fe, most Detours had at least two vehicles, so that one driver could help another when the inevitable breakdown occurred. When a vehicle eventually returned to the Santa Fe Garage, it was given a complete overnight mechanical checkup and a washing, so that it would be ready for the next day's Detour. Tires were checked and often replaced.

Drivers and Couriers sometimes fell in love on the long, lonely journey and several of them married, which was not prohibited by company rules after 1930. Fred Harvey figured that the employees would stay longer if they were happy and stabilized in their private lives. Drivers were paid $125/month and were allowed to accept tips from the dudes. Drivers were not allowed to drink alcohol, even when off duty. Vehicles were packed with blankets for the dudes, as well as water, coffee in thermoses, snacks, and basket lunches as there was often not a hotel or restaurant to stop at for lunch. Luggage was carried on the back of Harveycars and on the top of Harveycoaches. Car drivers were not allowed to be coach drivers unless they had special training in handling the large, heavy coaches.

With vehicles purchased, Couriers and Drivers hired and trained, it now fell to Fred Harvey to bring the La Fonda Hotel up to Harvey standards. "The Indian Detours were like a circular jigsaw puzzle ... the one piece at the center that the whole idea hinged on was the hotels. Without the assurance that the tourist would be well fed and have a good night's rest, many Detourists would never have bought a ticket."[16] The AT&SF brought in their company architect, Mary Colter, to decorate the interior of La Fonda.

Above left: La Plazuela dining room at La Fonda with its hand-painted glass windows is a very popular place to eat in Santa Fe.

Above right: The huge fireplace in La Fonda behind La Plazuela dining room was created by artist Arnold Ronnebeck incorporating symbols and characters from Zuni and Hopi tribal stories.

> Colter designed each hotel room individually, adding special touches such as hand-painted windows, hand-crafted light fixtures, and painted furniture ... Rooms were further decorated with original paintings by prominent Southwestern native artists ... The lobby and shared spaces were decorated with original paintings by Gerald Cassidy and murals by Olive Rush."[17]

"The Indian Detours became so immediately popular that La Fonda's fifty-five rooms were not sufficient."[18] Overflow guests were sent to Fred Harvey's El Ortiz Hotel in Lamy (opened in 1910) and to the AT&SF Pullman sleeper railroad cars parked at Lamy for that purpose. An expansion for La Fonda was soon planned. Mary Colter worked with local Santa Fe architect John Gaw Meem to expand the hotel to 180 rooms. Construction began late in 1926 and was completed in 1929.

> The genius of the (Fred Harvey) company that created La Fonda as we know it today was the ability to invent restaurants and hotels that felt as if they always had been a cozy part of the community, even on their opening day. They were like art and history museums where you could sleep over.[19]

Walking into La Fonda today, visitors will immediately realize the truth of that statement.

La Fonda Hotel is seen in this photograph when the expansion was completed in 1930. The view is from the corner of Water Street (right) and Old Santa Fe Trail (left). [*New Mexico History Museum exhibit*]

A contemporary view of La Fonda shows not a lot of change from 1930 at the same two street corners.

2

Promoting the Southwest and the Indian Detours

While the initial novelty of the Indian Detours assured their success in 1926, Fred Harvey and the AT&SF realized that future success would rely on extensive publicity.

> After that successful first summer of the Indian Detours, both Fred Harvey and the Santa Fe railroad began investing even more heavily in southwestern tourism. They also dramatically increased the use of Indian imagery to brand their companies.[1]

The Indians actually had very little say in the matter though. "The Pueblo Indians of New Mexico might well have preferred to remain in the relative seclusion they had enjoyed before the railroad era, but they had no voice in the matter."[2] The Indian imagery for publicity was often supplied by the local artists of Taos and Santa Fe. E. Alexander Powell visited Taos in the early 1910s, and:

> Powell asserted that in the footsteps of the frontiersman "have come another breed of men, who carry palettes instead of pistols and who confront the Indian with brushes instead of bowie knives; for Taos because of its extraordinary wealth of sun and shadows, of yellow deserts and purple mesas, of scarlet blankets and white walls, has become the rendezvous for a group of brilliant painters who are perpetuating on canvas the red men of the terraced houses."[3]

This group of brilliant painters was the Taos Society of Artists founded in 1915. One of its founding members was artist Eanger Irving Couse. Couse used Native models from Taos Pueblo in his paintings. Couse and other artists supported themselves in part by selling their paintings to the AT&SF for their advertising purposes.

> As one of the major contributors to western expansion, the Santa Fe's use of art for promotion was particularly effective in opening up the west to the tourist trade ... The implications of this ... are fundamental to understanding the relationship that developed between the railroad and Couse, whose paintings were used exclusively on the Santa Fe calendars from 1914 until 1938.[4]

In 2015 the town of Taos celebrated the 100th anniversary of the founding of the Taos Society of Artists on July 15, 1915, with this promotional postcard featuring the six founding artists. From left to right are J. H. Sharp, E. L. Blumenschein, W. H. Dunton, E. I. Couse, B. G. Phillips, and O. E. Berninghaus.

This painting by Taos artist E. I. Couse was titled "The Turquoise Maker," and was featured in the AT&SF calendar for 1959.

In 1900, William Haskell Simpson became the general advertising agent for the AT&SF. In his role he heavily promoted "advertising art" and told an interviewer:

> I think that we were the first railroad in the land to take art seriously, as a valuable advertising adjunct. We have never skimped. We use the very best art that can be bought, and we reproduce it in the very best way that it can be reproduced.[5]

That "very best art" was indeed an accurate description, as paintings by Taos Society of Artists sold at auction today often bring in prices in the hundreds of thousands of dollars. Simpson knew what he wanted in his advertising art, and he communicated directly with the artists to achieve his goals. "Simpson often participated in Couse's execution of a canvas. He would suggest alterations that would make the work more suitable for the purposes of the railway's advertising policy."[6]

Besides using Indian figures in advertising, the AT&SF promoted the incredible landscape of New Mexico and Arizona to tourists. From Carlsbad Caverns and Chaco Canyon in New Mexico to Monument Valley, Canyon de Chelly and the Grand Canyon in Arizona, these natural features were promoted heavily in Fred Harvey/AT&SF postcards and brochures.

> The Santa Fe had the right-of-way through some of the most astonishing scenery in creation. By emphasizing it, the railroad set about its task of mining the landscape for culture, the culture for artifacts, and the country for tourist traffic … It promoted tourism as the new religion … The railway's advertising images of the landscape and the Indian were glazed with beauty and picturesqueness, promoting a last refuge of magic, mountains and quaint ancestors.[7]

While the AT&SF promoted Indians and landscapes, Fred Harvey promoted Indian artifacts of the Southwest—weavings, pottery, jewelry, and baskets. Its ace in this area was a man called Herman Schweizer. Schweizer, born in Germany in 1871, emigrated to the United States in 1885. By the time he was seventeen years old, he became manager of the Harvey House dining room in Gallup, New Mexico.

> Herman Schweizer was like a character out of *Blazing Saddles*—a short, stocky, prematurely balding, cigar-chomping German-Jewish immigrant whose hobby was riding by horseback to Navajo trading posts and villages to buy or trade blankets, pottery, and jewelry … (he) spent much of his free time in Ganado, Arizona, fifty miles northwest of Gallup, where there were a handful of trading posts run by non-Indians … Schweizer learned everything he could about Indian art and culture … He (became) one of the few non-Indian experts in Navajo blankets, baskets, pottery, and especially jewelry.[8]

Meanwhile, Ford Harvey and his sister, Minnie Harvey Huckel, became intensely interested in the Indian arts and crafts of the Southwest. They decided to establish an "Indian Museum and Sales Room" at the Alvarado Hotel which opened in Albuquerque in 1902. They enlisted Herman Schweizer to purchase artifacts for the museum. Schweizer purchased Native arts from trading posts throughout the Southwest, including J. L. Hubbell's trading post in Ganado and L. C. Smith's trading post in Thoreau, New Mexico. He bought every collection of the highest value that he could find.

Above left: The June 11, 1939, Timetables brochure of the AT&SF featured the spectacular scenery of the Grand Canyon, along with tourists descending into the Canyon on mules and Indians peering out from the rim.

Above right: The 1932 brochure for the Indian Detours featured fantastic scenery from the Monument Valley in Arizona, along with the AT&SF logo and the Fred Harvey thunderbird logo, with a Harveycar motoring through the scenery. At the bottom left an Indian is shown holding a pot and at the bottom right Taos Pueblo is depicted.

> Significant collections for both the museum and sales room were acquired from trader John Lorenzo Hubbell of Ganado. Extensive orders of textiles were acquired from Hubbell along with purchases of jewelry, pottery, and basketry. These objects were transported by wagon from the trading post at Ganado to the train depot in Gallup (52 miles).[9]

From Gallup the AT&SF transported the artifacts to Albuquerque and the Alvarado. There, aspiring architect and Indian arts aficionado, Mary Colter, was brought in to set up the rooms in the museum with the artifacts purchased by Schweizer. Colter had attended the California School of Design in San Francisco, and while there had made the acquaintance of a Fred Harvey cashier who recommended her to the main Harvey office in Kansas City.

Above left: J. L. Hubbell trades for a Navajo blanket in front of his trading Post in Ganado, Arizona, in the 1890s. [*National Park Service*]

Above right: This photograph of the L. C. Smith trading post in Thoreau, New Mexico, c. 1915, is featured on the wall of the Shiprock Santa Fe gallery in Santa Fe with a shelf of artifacts for sale in front of the photograph.

> In 1902 ... Fred Harvey opened the Indian Room trackside at the new Alvarado Hotel in Albuquerque. Designed as a small Native Art museum, it quickly became a major tourist draw and retail business—largely because Mary Colter, with her background in both art and retail display, created dioramas that demonstrated ways in which blankets, baskets, pottery, and other cultural artifacts commonly seen in spare Native American homes could be exhibited more lushly ... Ironically, this combination of craftsmanship and decoration which most tourists first saw in Albuquerque at the train station museum, became known as Santa Fe style.[10]

But it was Santa Fe that became the hub of the Indian Detours, not Albuquerque, so the term "Santa Fe Style" turned out to be appropriate.

Fred Harvey and Schweizer soon realized that tourists could not take large Native pots, baskets, and heavy jewelry home with them in their luggage on the train. So, Schweizer developed a "Navajo-lite" style. Just as William Haskell Simpson "manipulated" artist paintings for AT&SF calendars, so Schweizer encouraged Native artists to "downsize" their works. Large water pots carried on the heads of Native women were downsized to hand-size pots the dudes could take home with them. Heavy Navajo jewelry was made with lighter-weight silver and cheaper turquoise. "As early as 1899, Schweizer sought lighter-weight silver jewelry to suit customer desires, and he supplied cut and polished Nevada turquoise to a trader in Thoreau New, New Mexico, for use in Native-crafted

Above left: The Indian Building in front of the Alvarado Hotel in Albuquerque c. 1910 with tourists perusing the crafts for sale from Indians on the sidewalk. Inside, the museum and sales room were decorated by Mary Colter. [*Library of Congress, LC-USZ62-97656*]

Above right: The Indian Building was still intact, but abandoned, in 1969, just before its demolition along with the Alvarado Hotel in 1970. [*Library of Congress, HABS NM, 1-ALBU, 5-123-21*]

jewelry."[11] Schweizer also thought that the Navajo textiles should be more colorful to appeal to the dudes. He "specified colors and materials in the Navajo textiles that were acquired from Hubbell and sold in Harvey establishments, strongly opposing the use of cotton for the foundation fibers in Navajo rugs" insisting that only wool was to be used.[12]

While Schweizer and Fred Harvey did change the substance of Native arts and crafts in the Southwest, the Natives seemed happy to comply, as the objects they sold brought much needed cash to their pueblos and hogans.

> Whether a demonstration of pueblo life or an invasion of privacy, the Harvey Detours were key to the Pueblos financial well-being. Sales of arts and crafts to visitors was an important source of cash as the pueblos adjusted to twentieth-century economics.[13]

As Edmund Ladd of Zuni Pueblo noted, "We've gone from ritual to retail."[14]

Besides influencing paintings and Native arts and crafts for promotional purposes, AT&SF/Fred Harvey created thousands of advertising brochures for the railroad and for the Indian Detours. When the Indian Detours began in 1926, AT&SF publicist Roger Birdseye "claimed that some two million pieces of Santa Fe printed matter are absorbed annually by the general public." These printed pieces included postcards, calendars, matchbooks, playing cards, dining menus, and brochures for the Indian Detours.

Native imagery was heavily used in these promotional pieces.

> Very quickly, the Santa Fe and Fred Harvey companies both saw the advantages of using images of Native peoples in their advertising. In contrast to the popular misconception

The large utilitarian water-carrying pot of this Santa Clara Pueblo woman was much too large to sell to Detourists seeking smaller souvenirs to take home with them. So, Fred Harvey personnel encouraged the Natives to make smaller pots to sell. [*Photograph by Carl Moon, c. 1910, PhotCL313(224), Huntington Library*]

> of Native Americans as brutal warriors, they were presented as the "exotic other" to attract rail travelers. By 1901, the Santa Fe used Native imagery widely in promoting travel to entice travelers away from Europe and toward the Southwest.[16]

Using this Native imagery for advertising purposes was still somewhat risky for AT&SF at this time, as the Indian battles on the Western frontier had only finished ten years prior with the Battle of Wounded Knee on December 29, 1890. However, the Natives of the Southwest were portrayed as peaceful, sedentary people living quiet lives in pueblos. AT&SF/Fred Harvey advertising used photographs and paintings of nearly all the pueblo people and tribes of the Southwest.

The first Indian Detour brochure was published by the AT&SF in November 1925 to promote the start of the Detours in the spring of 1926. "This publication became an annual brochure containing updated information on excursion prices and a variety of tours for tourists to choose from."[17] The success of the Indian Detours campaign is difficult to measure because most of the AT&SF records were lost to a fire in their Topeka office in the 1940s. However, "the increase in hotels and curio shops (in the Southwest) between 1920 and 1940 may be a testament to the marketing efforts of the AT&SF and the Harvey Company."[18] Also, the tourist industry today is one of the largest contributors to the economy of New Mexico and Arizona, and:

> is directly traceable to the ideals of hospitality fostered by the Fred Harvey Company. Our assumption of effortless travel among widely separated, remote destinations harkens back to the days of easy transportation by rail. Sustained promotions through (AT&SF/Fred Harvey) advertising alerted travelers to the attractions of one of America's most remote regions.[19]

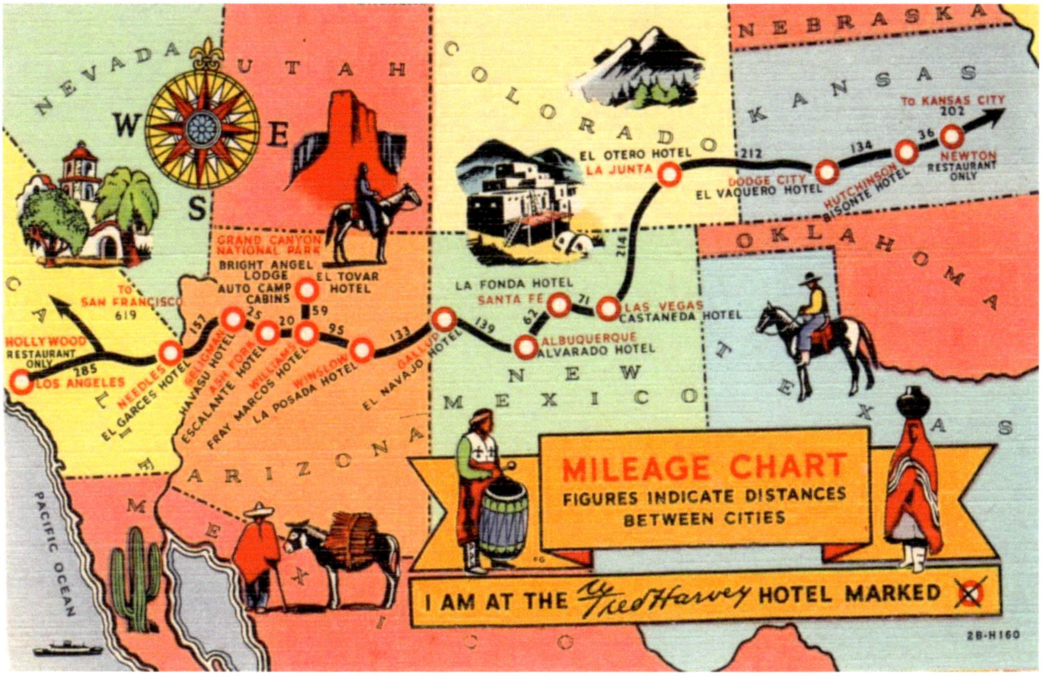

Above: One example of the thousands of postcards that Fred Harvey produced to advertise their hotels and restaurants. Travelers could mark the hotel they were staying at and then post the card to family or friends. Notice the many examples of Indian imagery on the card.

Right: This ad for the "Indian-detour" using Native imagery, appeared in *The Literary Digest* issue for May 15, 1926, the first day of operation of the Detours. A young Native boy is pounding on a drum with the AT&SF logo prominent in the background.

This cover of the La Fonda Hotel Fred Harvey lunch menu featured Native and Hispanic imagery as well as advertising the Indian Detour. [*New Mexico History Museum exhibit*]

The 1928 brochure for the Indian Detours again featured Native imagery with a blanket-covered figure sitting next to a ladder which leads down into a kiva. There is also a Native pot, two Native figures next to the Harveycoach, and a Pueblo in the lower right background. Notice the AT&SF passenger train smoking along tracks in the lower left background.

3

The First Indian Detours

With planning firmed up for the start of the Indian Detours in May of 1926, the news was given to the press in August 1925, to start drumming up interest in the tours. The *Albuquerque Morning Journal* report of August 20, 1925, was nothing short of ecstatic with the headline "Santa Fe Will Establish Bus Detour Through Indian Pueblos—Most Interesting Country in America."[1] The news article went on to state:

> The Santa Fe Railway system announced here Wednesday the establishment of an Indian detour rail and motor-way which will enable rail tourists from Chicago to California to see points of historic and scenic interest in this state ... the best New Mexico ... has to offer in the way of interest to the sightseer ... spending three days traveling by auto bus through the mountains, valleys, canyons and Indian Pueblos of this section of the southwest ... It will be an all-expense motor trip under Santa Fe-Fred Harvey management covering nearly 300 miles of auto transportation, as well as meals and hotel accommodations enroute ... The announcement is considered one of the most important ever made in modern railroading in that for the first time in history a transportation system will be operating a rail and bus system in parallel lines over a great part of its territory.[2]

Those parallel lines would eventually run from Raton, New Mexico, to the Grand Canyon in Arizona, with numerous side trips available. The 1926 brochure emphasized that fact as it "suggested indulging in private trips in one of the luxurious Packards, branching out into Arizona and Colorado."[3] The brochure was optimistic in spelling out the details of the three-day Indian Detour since the Harvey Company did not even initiate a trial run until March 27, 1926, only a month and a half before the Detours were scheduled to begin.

> "A trial automobile detour was run ... from Albuquerque to Santa Fe to Las Vegas; the roads were terrible, the journey was long and difficult, but with Harvey food and Harvey accommodations at the Alvarado, La Fonda, and the Castañeda, the trip was a success and the Southwestern Indian Detours were officially begun.[4]

With stomachs full of delicious Fred Harvey breakfast, the first Detourists set out from the Castañeda Hotel in Las Vegas, New Mexico, on May 15, 1926. A Harveycar and a Harveycoach carried the passengers southwest through Kearny's Gap and deep into Hispanic New Mexico. The Couriers pointed out that Kearny's Gap was named after U.S. General Stephen Watts Kearny, who led the American army west through the gap in the hills on August 17, 1846, on to Santa Fe to engage the Mexican army in battle. Upon entering Santa Fe, Kearny discovered that the Mexicans had fled, and Kearny took the city without a shot being fired. The war soon ended, and America gained as a prize the entire Southwest from New Mexico to Arizona to California. Kearny's Gap is not the cut seen on today's Interstate 25 south of Las Vegas. The Gap is about two miles to the north on New Mexico Highway 283.

After Kearny's Gap, the Detourists soon entered the small Hispanic town of Tecolote, where the Couriers explained that *tecolote* was the Spanish word for "owl," and that Tecolote Peak was seen four miles north of town. It is difficult to imagine the wonder with which these eastern dudes must have first glimpsed a Hispanic village of adobe homes with flat roofs, canales, and vigas. The canales were cut into parapets on the roof so that water would drain off. The vigas were sturdy pine logs that supported the roof, and they projected out from under the parapets. While this sight must have initially dazzled the Detourists, they would soon become used to this construction method seen throughout New Mexico, Arizona, and the Indian Pueblos.

Next stop for the Detourists heading west was the small village of San Jose where there was an old Spanish mission church for them to explore. San Jose was an important stop on the Santa Fe Trail as there was a shallow crossing of the Pecos River there.

Continuing on west, the Harveycars brought the dudes to the Pecos Ruins. On a hill overlooking the Pecos River,

> during the Classic Period (1325–1600), the many 50–100+ pueblos that had once dotted the landscape began to consolidate into one larger settlement at Pecos Pueblo by 1450 ... Pecos Pueblo hosted a lively trade between the Plains Indians and the Rio Grande Pueblos.[5]

While Pecos Pueblo was very prosperous from this trade, the next trade period spelled doom for the pueblo. This was the Santa Fe Trail which went right through Pueblo land. The traders and settlers on this trail brought diseases which decimated the Natives. By 1838 the few remaining Pecos people migrated eighty miles west to Jemez Pueblo, where they joined their Towa-speaking relatives. Pecos Pueblo was completely abandoned and looted of its stones and timbers. The remains which are seen there today are the stone foundation of the pueblo and the Catholic church which was built in 1717. When the Detourists visited in 1926 the Couriers provided the descriptive narrative, since the New Mexico state monument at Pecos was not established until 1935, and the National Park Service national monument not until 1965. Eventually the Pecos National Historical Park was established in 1990 with the addition of the Forked Lightning Ranch and the Glorieta Civil War Battlefields to the park boundaries.

About six miles north of Pecos Pueblo, the Detourists stopped at the Apache Inn at the Valley Ranch for lunch. Fred Harvey made sure the food there met Harvey standards. After an hour for lunch, it was back into the Harveycar and coach to continue the journey along the Santa Fe Trail west to Glorieta Pass at 7,432 feet. This was a

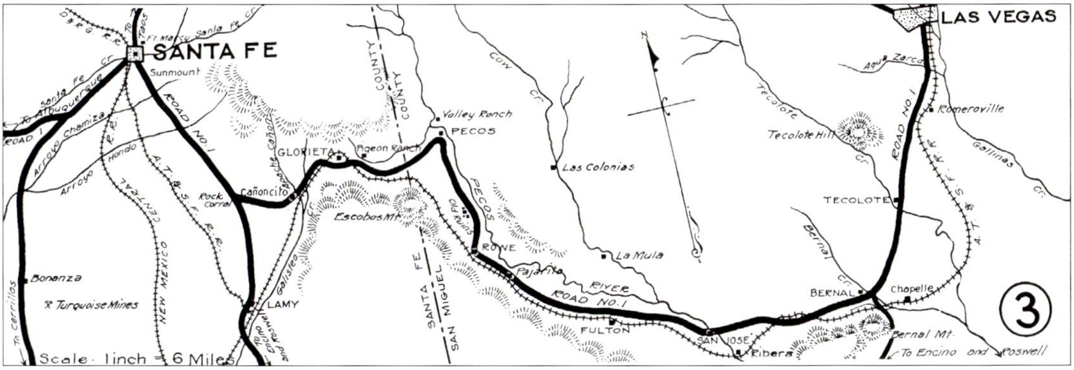

This map from an early Detours brochure shows the route of the first Indian Detour from Las Vegas to Tecolote, San Jose, Pecos, Valley Ranch, Glorieta Pass, and Cañoncito to Santa Fe. Note the location of Lamy in relation to Santa Fe.

Kearny's Gap is seen in 2023 along New Mexico Highway 283 just south of Las Vegas.

The ruins of an adobe home are seen in Tecolote in 2023.

Above left: San Jose Plaza is seen in 2023 along the original Indian Detour route which followed the Santa Fe Trail across a shallow ford of the Pecos River outside San Jose.

Above right: The Detourists visited this Catholic church in San Jose on the first Indian Detour in 1926. It is still in good condition nearly 100 years later in 2023.

The church ruins at Pecos were photographed by Frederick Nichols *circa* 1924, just before the Detourists arrived at the site in 1926. [*Library of Congress, HABS, NM, 24-PECO,1*]

The ruins at Pecos have been stabilized by the National Park Service and look much the same today as they did in 1926.

trading center and loading station for the AT&SF in the Sangre de Cristo Mountains. Descending west from the pass into Apache Canyon the dudes would see the AT&SF tracks on their left, and the little church at Cañoncito on their right.

The road then climbed up out of the canyon to Santa Fe and their night's lodging at La Fonda. However, the day was not done for the weary travelers, as they were given a conducted tour of the Indian Museum and Art Gallery before dinner. After dinner they attended a "lecture by School of American Research on the history, arts, crafts and quaint ceremonials of the Pueblo Indians"[6] which they would soon be witnessing.

After a relaxing night's sleep at La Fonda, the Detourists headed out the next morning at 9 a.m. for Tesuque Pueblo, six miles north of Santa Fe, just west of the distinctive Camel Rock formation. This would be their first introduction to live Natives in a pueblo. Tesuque was a very small pueblo with a limited arts and crafts tradition. It had played a major role in the Pueblo Revolt of 1680 where the pueblos of New Mexico rose up united to drive their hated Spanish conquerors back to Mexico. "Tesuque struck the first blows of the revolt. They were the first to kill a public official and the first to do in a priest."[7] Most of the original Spanish churches built in the Pueblos across New Mexico were destroyed in the revolt. By 1692, the Spanish had reconquered the Pueblos, and they began rebuilding the churches. The small church seen by the Detourists in Tesuque is the San Diego mission church built in 1915. The church can be seen in the upper left of the Tesuque photograph on page 40."

> By 1920, traditional pottery was history at Tesuque, and production had switched over to mass manufacture of rain gods, strange little creatures that look like space aliens holding buckets between their legs ... (they were) sold as sacred ceremonial items, but they were the furthest thing from them.[8]

At Glorieta Pass today the AT&SF train station has been transformed into a U.S. post office.

The church at Cañoncito, constructed in the late 1800s, was seen by the Detourists as the road came west out of Apache Canyon and headed up to Santa Fe. The adobe church is Nuestra Señora de la Luz, "Our Lady of the Light."

The AT& SF Super Chief streamliner has left Lamy and is headed east into Apache Canyon at Cañoncito in the 1950s.

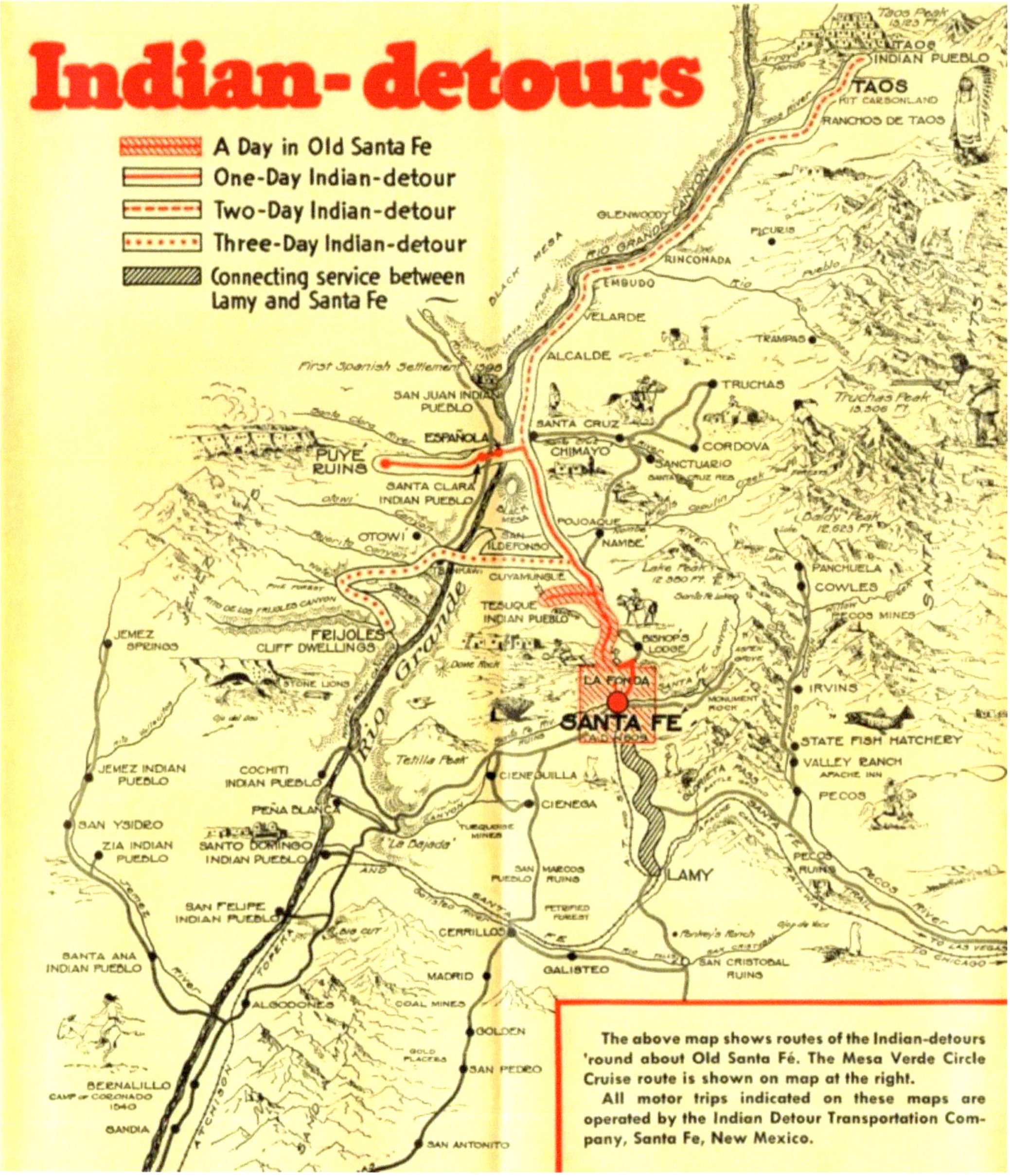

Relaxing overnight at La Fonda in Santa Fe, the Detourists could study this map showing their next day's journey to Tesuque Pueblo, Puye Ruins, Santa Clara Pueblo, and San Juan Pueblo.

The Detourists were only allowed fifteen minutes at Tesuque, just enough time to take a picture of the church and purchase a rain god. If the Detourists had had enough time and arrived on the right day, they might have seen something that *was* a sacred ceremonial at Tesuque—a performance of the Eagle Dance or the Buffalo Dance. The Eagle Dance was a prayer for healing and could be performed at any time of the year.

> This is because eagles are always strong, so they can cure anything ... (the dance) requires unusual skill and an amazing control of leg muscles in its stooping, swooping, varied movements...danced by only two men...The striking feature of the costume is the wings. Each arm is feathered from shoulder to fingers with the real quills of the eagle's wing.[9]

The Buffalo Dance was performed at several pueblos, including Tesuque. It represents a prayer for successful hunting of wild game—buffalo, deer, and elk. "The buffalo are played by two men whose bodies, naked above the waist, are painted black, as are their faces under the heavy shaggy buffalo heads."[10] It was a complicated dance, but in general, a beautiful young woman dancer goes out into the hills to lure the wild game into the plaza where male dancers with bow and arrow kill it.

From Tesuque Pueblo, the Indian Detour proceeded north to Española for a quick coffee break, before turning southwest to the ruins at Puye. The Detourists were allowed one hour to explore the Indian ruins there. Puye has ruins of cave dwellings in the cliffside and ruins of a pueblo on the mesa top. To reach the top, the dudes had to climb a steep ladder on the cliff face. To accomplish all this in one hour was nearly impossible, so the tour was inevitably late for its next stop at Santa Clara Pueblo. "The Santa Clara Indians say their ancestors lived in the winter in the caves excavated in the pumice cliffs and in the pueblo on the mesa above in the summer."[11] Tree-ring dating reveals that Puye was built between 1450 and 1475 and was at its height in 1540. Up to 1,500 people lived in the pueblo. "A major drought forced the inhabitants to abandon Puye in the sixteenth century. The people moved down canyon to a more reliable water source, the Rio Grande."[12] The pueblo established along the Rio Grande was named Santa Clara. The Spanish gave the pueblos names of various saints, and today many pueblos are switching their name to their native language name. In a curious mixing of cultures, "all the Rio Grande Pueblos dance on the day of the saint for whom the Spaniards named their village."[13] From Puye it was a steep ten-mile descent for the Harveycar drivers down the canyon on a gravel road to the next stop at Santa Clara Pueblo.

Santa Clara Pueblo has been located on the west bank of the Rio Grande since about 1600. The adobe church seen by the Detourists there was built in 1918. The tour allowed for a stop of only twenty minutes at Santa Clara, hardly time for the dudes to admire the outstanding display of pottery offered by the artisans on the plaza. Santa Clarans "really make pottery. Perhaps 200 Santa Clara potters are turning out stylish blackware and redware, including some of the highest priced pottery ever made."[14]

From Santa Clara it was a quick five-minute drive north to Española for lunch. By now it was 1:00 p.m. or later and the dudes had really worked up an appetite. Unfortunately, the food offered at the hotel in Española never measured up to Fred Harvey standards. Frustrated, Fred Harvey then contracted lunch service with pueblo women cooks at Santa Clara, and this was an improvement, but not a long-term solution. The solution

Above left: The Eagle Dance at Tesuque was photographed by Edward Kemp c. 1927. Kemp was a commercial photographer based in San Francisco, who along with his wife, Josephine, traveled throughout the Southwest, photographing the Hopi Snake Dance, and other Pueblo Indian dances and scenes.

Above right: Edward S. Curtis photographed the Buffalo Dance at Tesuque, c. 1927. [*Library of Congress, LC-USZ62-97087*]

Edward Kemp was on the scene at the Puye Ruins photographing the Detourists, c. 1927. Note the Detourist driver with the Stetson hat chatting with the gentleman on the right.

The rest house at Puye was constructed by Fred Harvey in 1927 to serve lunch to the Detourists when lunch facilities in Española proved inadequate. [*Photograph from 1930 Indian Detours brochure*]

The Puye cliff dwellings and rest house make for an interesting stop on the drive from Santa Fe today.

Santa Clara Pueblo looking south to Black Mesa with the Rio Grande in the mid-distance. [*Photograph by John Hillers, 1880, Phot.CL190(2), Huntington Library*]

At Santa Clara Pueblo, Natives display their pottery for sale next to a Harveycar. [*Photograph by Edward Kemp, circa 1927*]

Several Harveycars parked at Santa Clara Pueblo, c. 1930. It is clear to see why some pueblo residents would feel overwhelmed by the crowds of tourists. [*New Mexico History Museum exhibit*]

The current adobe church at Santa Clara Pueblo was constructed in August 1918. It replaced earlier churches, the first destroyed in the Pueblo Revolt of 1680, and subsequent structures which collapsed.

was to build a facility at Puye, and Fred Harvey constructed a stone rest house there in 1927, where picnic lunches or warm food could be served to the Detourists. Puye is a part of the Santa Clara reservation, and this was the only facility that Fred Harvey ever constructed on an Indian reservation.

After lunch, the Detourists moved on to San Juan Pueblo, just a few miles north of Española on the east bank of the Rio Grande. Today the pueblo goes by its Tewa name, "Ohkay Owingeh." While Zuni Pueblo speaks its own language, the other pueblos of New Mexico speak four different languages as follows: Tewa (pronounced Tay-wah) is spoken at San Juan, Santa Clara, San Ildefonso, Pojoaque, Nambe and Tesuque; Tiwa (pronounced Tee-wah) is spoken at Taos, Picuris, Sandia, and Isleta Pueblos; Towa is the language of Jemez Pueblo and the Pecos Puebloans who migrated to Jemez; the Keres language is spoken at Cochiti, Santo Domingo, San Felipe, Santa Ana, Zia, Laguna, and Acoma Pueblos. The ancient languages are much less frequently spoken today, as most Puebloans speak Spanish and English.

Ohkay Owingeh is more known for its role in the Spanish history of New Mexico than it is for pottery or other crafts. It was the site of the first Spanish settlement in New Mexico in 1598, but finding the natives unfriendly, the Spanish moved west across the Rio Grande from the pueblo and established their own settlement at San Gabriel. This became the first capital of the territory until the permanent capital was established in Santa Fe in 1610. San Juan Pueblo was the birthplace of Po'Pay leader of the Pueblo Revolt in 1680. The red-brick church seen in the plaza by the Detourists in 1926 is San Juan Bautista, built in 1913.

The Detourists left San Juan Pueblo about 3:00 p.m. for a 4:00 p.m. arrival back at La Fonda in Santa Fe. After an hour of rest, it was back in the cars and buses for a one-hour tour of Santa Fe. Dinner was at the hotel at 6:00 p.m., but that was not the end

San Juan Pueblo (now known as Ohkay-Ohwingeh) looking west to the church and the Pajarito Plateau. [*Photograph by John Hillers, 1880, Phot.CL190(10), Huntington Library*]

Above: Corn drying on the top of adobe homes at San Juan Pueblo. [*Photograph by John Hillers, 1880, Phot.CL190(8), Huntington Library*]

Right: The San Juan Caballero church in San Juan Pueblo today is a brick structure which replaced the old adobe church demolished 1912.

of the day's activities, as an "Indian Play" was scheduled in the St. Francis Auditorium of the New Mexico Art Museum at 8:00 p.m. Fred Harvey wanted to be sure that guests received their money's worth for their $45.00 three-day Detour.

On the third day, the Detourists headed from Santa Fe to Albuquerque departing La Fonda at 9:00 a.m., reaching Santo Domingo Pueblo at 10:15 a.m. after a hair-raising drive over the switchbacks on La Bajada Hill. An hour and a half stop was scheduled at Santo Domingo, so if Detourists were there on August 4, perhaps they could see part of the Corn Dance. This dance was a prayer for rain and growth of the crops. The dance is also known as the Tablita Dance, referring to the head-dresses worn by the women.

> There are often as many as two hundred dancers, perfectly costumed and trained like an operatic chorus ... the tablitas are thin board plaques, painted turquoise blue, the sky color, and cut at the top into shapes of mesa and cloud.[15]

Santo Domingo (Saint Dominic) Pueblo was established in the fifteenth century by immigrants from the Pajarito Plateau to the north when it suffered severe drought. This was the same drought that drove the Puyans down to Santa Clara, and the natives of Tsankawi down to San Ildefonso. However, Santo Domingo was beset by floods from the Rio Grande, and their village was destroyed three times until finally settling into its present location about 1886. Santo Domingo artisans are more known for their jewelry than for pottery. They were known "as the best of the Pueblo beadmakers."[16] Their beads were called *heishi*, which is a Keres word for "shell." Shell and turquoise were used in their beadmaking.

Leaving Santo Domingo, the Detourists would arrive at the Alvarado Hotel in Albuquerque about 12:45 p.m. where lunch was served. This would allow for a leisurely lunch and rest as the next tour did not leave until 3:00 p.m. for Isleta Pueblo. Isleta's historic pueblo is about eight miles south of Albuquerque on the west bank of the Rio Grande, while today's Isleta casino is on the east bank. Being close to Albuquerque has always had its advantages and disadvantages. The disadvantage was that the Spanish

The switchbacks on La Bajada Hill southwest of Santa Fe provided a hair-raising ride for the Detourists as this 1926 photograph illustrates. [*Library of Congress, LOC-HAER NM-7*]

The *estufa* (kiva ceremonial chamber) at Santo Domingo Pueblo was photographed by Carl Moon in 1904. Ceremony participants climbed up the ladder and then down into the chamber. Moon was hired by Fred Harvey in 1907 to take photographs of Southwest Indians for publicity materials. [*Phot.CL313(210), Huntington Library*]

The Corn Dance at Santo Domingo Pueblo had a lot of participants and onlookers in this scene from 1904. [*Photograph by Carl Moon, 1904, Phot.CL313(212), Huntington Library*]

Above left: Edward S. Curtis photographed this female Tablita dancer at San Ildefonso Pueblo, c. 1905. The Tablita headdress was worn by females at the various pueblo Corn Dances, including the dance at Santo Domingo. [*Library of Congress, LC-USZ62-115816*]

Above right: Notice the female dancers with tablita headdresses in the Corn Dance with the men dancers at Santa Domingo Pueblo. [*Photograph by Carl Moon, 1904, Phot.CL313(209), Huntington Library*]

army in Albuquerque could maintain control of the pueblo, and so Isleta did not participate in the Pueblo Revolt of 1680, the only pueblo not to do so. And while Isleta has historically been a farming community, its proximity to Albuquerque has offered many job opportunities in the modern era. Isletans are proud of their Saint Augustine church, built in 1716 and still standing today. The Isleta feast day is dedicated to Saint Augustine and held annually on September 4, usually accompanied by a harvest dance. "Probably the best known of all Isleta arts is its Indian breadbaking; loaves are baked daily in small beehive-shaped mud ovens called 'hornos' and sold to visitors for about $2.00 a loaf."[17] The fresh bread would come out of the ovens early in the morning, so unfortunately the Detourists missed out on this treat.

After the tour of Isleta, the Detourists were chauffeured back to Albuquerque for a drive around the city, arriving at the Alvarado for dinner about 5:30 p.m. At 7:00 p.m., a tour of the adjacent Fred Harvey Indian Building was scheduled, and the Detourists could marvel at the decorating skill of Mary Colter and the many Indian arts and crafts purchased by Herman Schweizer offered for sale. Many souvenirs were grabbed here, placed in Detourist suitcases, and loaded with passengers the next day on the westbound AT&SF train, thus concluding a highly successful three-day Indian Detour in 1926.

A fine overview of Isleta Pueblo taken c. 1890 by an unknown photographer. Notice the Saint Augustine Church in the background. [*Phot. 215(51), Huntington Library*]

This New Year's Dance at Isleta Pueblo was captured by an unknown photographer c. 1890. Notice the snow on the ground. [*Phot. 215(57), Huntington Library*]

Left: Carl Moon photographed Isleta Pueblo woman, Juana Marie, in her traditional dress, c. 1904. She is fully adorned with squash blossom necklace, bracelets, and leg wrappings which are attached to her moccasins. [*Phot. CL313(204), Huntington Library*]

Below: Carl Moon photographed Isleta women baking bread in a horno oven in 1907. [*Phot. CL313(217), Huntington Library*]

4

Detours from Santa Fe: Roads to Yesterday

The Indian Detours were operated by the Santa Fe Transportation Company under the direction of Hunter Clarkson.

> The Santa Fe Transportation company is the "Harvey Indian Detour" system of scenic travels in New Mexico, Colorado and Arizona ... The Fred Harvey Company and the Santa Fe Transportation Company are separate corporations, but they work on a co-operative basis in the "Harvey Indian Detour" projects.[1]

The three-day Indian Detours of 1926 were so successful that 1927 saw the addition of one-day tours on the "Roads to Yesterday." These tours could be added on to the three-day Detour, or they could be a stand-alone day trip. The reference to "Roads to Yesterday" was to the many Indian ruins and Native pueblos which could be seen in one day from Santa Fe. These included the ruins at Bandelier and Puye, and the pueblos of Tesuque, San Ildefonso, Santa Clara, San Juan, and Taos. They also included the historic Hispanic villages of Chimayo, Cordova, and Truchas. Each was no more than forty miles from Santa Fe, though Taos was sixty-five miles and overnight accommodations could be acquired there at the Don Fernando Hotel.

San Ildefonso Pueblo was only twenty-five miles north of Santa Fe, so it was easily just a half-day trip which could be combined with others. The attraction at San Ildefonso for the Detourists was the pottery, for this was the home of the famous potter Maria Martinez. "Around 1919, Maria Martinez and (husband) Julian perfected what would become the trademark San Ildefonso pottery, the lovely blackware (created by smothering the fire with manure)."[2] Maria's son Popovi Da and her grandson Tony Da carried on this tradition for many years. San Ildefonso is located on the east bank of the Rio Grande and had been established in the 1300s when the natives of Tsankawi on the Pajarito Plateau moved off the plateau due to drought.

Across the Rio Grande from San Ildefonso was a frame house owned by Maria and Julian Martinez. Their son Adam lived in this house when he was the freight agent for the Denver & Rio Grande Railroad's Chili Line stop here at Otowi. On May 1, 1928, Edith Warner became the freight agent, replacing Adam Martinez, and she moved into

Above left: A panoramic view of San Ildefonso Pueblo c. 1880 by John Hillers. The view is west toward the Rio Grande and the Pajarito Plateau. Notice the church in the upper middle. [*Phot. CL190(7), Huntington Library*]

Above right: Edward Kemp photographed the kiva at San Ildefonso Pueblo c. 1927 with a Harveycar, two drivers, and a courier, along with two Natives. Black Mesa is in the background.

Left: This January 2019 view at the entrance to San Ildefonso Pueblo shows new snow on the ground and on Black Mesa in the distance.

The San Ildefonso church was built in 1968 as a replica of the original 1717 church. The adobe church stands out brilliantly with snow all around in January 2019.

Harveycars pause to let the Detourists take in the view at Black Mesa on the San Ildefonso Reservation in this photograph from the 1930 Indian Detour brochure.

The one-lane bridge built in 1921 over the Rio Grande is shown here in January 2019 viewing east with the modern highway bridge to the left. The Detourists would have crossed this bridge heading west on their trip to Bandelier National Monument.

this house. "With the aid of Adam Martinez and his great-uncle Atilano Montoya, she was able to remodel the middle room into a tearoom where she could serve meals to her guests."[3] Edith served tea and her famous chocolate cake to tourists on their way up to Bandelier National Monument. The Indian Detours probably did not stop here, but the Detourists undoubtedly saw Edith's home as they rode over the one-lane bridge which had been constructed across the Rio Grande in 1921. The bridge and remains of Edith's home can still be seen today.

Next stop for the Detourists after San Ildefonso was Bandelier National Monument, high up on the Pajarito Plateau. AT&SF/Fred Harvey brochures often referred to this place as *Frijoles* which is the Spanish word for "beans."

> On February 11, 1916, President Woodrow Wilson declared 45 square miles of the Pajarito Plateau including Frijoles Canyon a national monument, naming it in honor of its best known advocate, Adolph F. Bandelier ... (in 1880) Bandelier became the first researcher to visit the long, narrow canyon on the eastern slopes of the Jemez Mountains which he called El Rito de Los Frijoles, guided by a Cochiti Indian (Adelaido Montoya).[4]

El Rito de Los Frijoles—the "little river of the beans"—referred to the stream which flows through the canyon, allowing cultivation of beans, corn, and squash, staples of the Pueblo Indians who lived at the village of Tyuonyi at the bottom of the canyon. The ruins of Tyuonyi and the hundreds of caves in the pumice cliffs were the attractions leading tourists to Bandelier. A major problem was access—the only way into the canyon was by a steep, winding trail one-and-a-half miles long from the top of the canyon rim to the bottom. There was a ranch at the bottom operated by Mr. & Mrs.

George Frey, which offered meals and refreshments in 1925. All the supplies had to come in via the trail. George Frey wanted to take the tourists on a drive along the canyon floor to see the ruins, so he "took apart a Dodge truck, carried the parts into the canyon and reassembled them. He also built a gasoline-powered cable car that ran from the canyon rim to the floor."[5]

The lack of a road into Bandelier was a continual headache for the Indian Detours. The trail meant a three-mile round trip hike for the dudes, most of whom were not used to high elevation. The dudes could usually make it into the canyon, but the hike back up often proved challenging, resulting in delays to the scheduling of the Harveycars' return to other locations. In 1931, the Detours brochure noted that on the Two-Day Indian Detour the "rate reduced from $40.00 to $35.00 per person … No change in type of service but routing altered to eliminate Frijoles Canyon."[6] The solution finally came with the arrival of the Civilian Conservation Corps (a Depression-era make-work program for unemployed young men) in 1933. At Bandelier, the CCC constructed a visitor center, maintenance building, a new lodge, dining room, and gift shop. These replaced the ranch facilities of Mr. & Mrs. Frey, but they continued as managers of the new lodge. Also:

> despite considerable opposition by those who feared an invasion of tourists and damage to natural surroundings, the CCC constructed a twelve-foot-wide road into the canyon … in the fall of 1933. The first car was driven down the long-awaited road on December 9, 1933.[7]

The road removed the headache for the Indian Detours, but eventually the fear of an "invasion of tourists" came to fruition. Today, so many tourists come to Bandelier that the parking lot in the canyon is overwhelmed in the summer, and visitors must now ride shuttle buses into the canyon during the busiest months.

Other Roads to Yesterday from Santa Fe led the Detourists to the small Hispanic communities of Chimayo, Cordova, and Truchas. They were about 25–30 miles north of Santa Fe and made for an interesting one-day Detour. Chimayo was a weaving center, and the dudes could admire the beautiful blankets produced there. Chimayo also had a famous church—El Santuario del Chimayo. The church was finished in 1816 by Don Bernardo Abeyta.

> Local legend has it that Abeyta unearthed a Guatemalan priest's crucifix, and by touching the soil surrounding it, he was healed of his afflictions. Abeyta built El Santuario on the site of the holy soil, and today, thousands of pilgrims come annually to Chimayo to visit the church and receive a sample of the healing soil from a room adjoining the church.[8]

A little farther north from Chimayo is Cordova, known for the Lopez family of wood carvers. In Cordova, the dudes stopped for a look at St. Anthony's Catholic Church, an adobe building constructed in 1832 with funds provided by Don Bernardo Abeyta of Chimayo.

Five miles north of Cordova is the little community of Truchas, named after the nearby Rio de las Truchas (river of trout). Here, the dudes could admire the scenery

The Cave Kiva at Bandelier National Monument was photographed by George Grant for the National Park Service in 1934. A visitor is climbing the ladder out of the kiva.

The Cave Kiva at Bandelier is located in a cave high on the cliff wall. Its entrance is now sealed at the top by a metal plate.

Above left: A sign at the bottom of the cliff warns visitors at Bandelier about the difficulty of climbing the series of four ladders up to the Cave Kiva. The ladders have no handrails, making it difficult for those with fear of heights to ascend.

Above right: After climbing two ladders up to the Cave Kiva, there is a bench where visitors can rest before ascending the final two ladders to the cave.

from the 8,000-foot-high plateau, with desert stretching out to the west and 13,000-foot peaks to the east. A short stroll through the village revealed the adobe church built in the early 1800s—Nuestra Señora del Rosario—Our Lady of the Rosary. After this pleasant journey to the Hispanic communities, the Detourists returned to the comforts of the La Fonda Hotel in Santa Fe.

The highlight of any Road to Yesterday Detour from Santa Fe would be the journey north to Taos. This was a difficult trip in the 1920s and '30s. The sixty-five-mile drive along the Rio Grande and the Rio Pueblo took about three hours, so it would have been more comfortable for the Detourists to stay overnight in Taos at the Don Fernando Hotel, rather than making the long journey back in the late afternoon. And there was so much to see in the Taos area—Ranchos de Taos with its historic church, the plaza in Taos with its shops and art galleries, and of course, Taos Pueblo at the north end of town.

The first stop for the Detourists was the San Francisco de Asis (St. Francis of Assisi) Church in the Ranchos de Taos Plaza. Ranchos de Taos was settled by Hispanic ranchers on the Cristobal de la Serna land grant in the 1730s, with a village taking shape by the

El Santuario de Chimayo is a beautiful place to visit any time of the year with large trees providing cool shade in the summer months.

Above left: Edward Kemp photographed the San Antonio de Padua church in Cordova c. 1927 with a Harveycar, two drivers in Stetson hats, and a courier at the gate with a Hispanic woman.

Above right: In Truchas the Detourists visited the Nuestra Señora del Rosario (Our Lady of the Rosary) church, which still stands today and has been restored.

Edward Kemp photographed this Harveycar and its passengers on their descent into the Rio Pueblo Canyon south of Taos.

The road through the Rio Pueblo Canyon was eventually paved and served as the main road into Taos from the south until the road was destroyed by rockslides in the 1950s. Visitors today can hike the Slide Trail along the old road (seen upper left) into the canyon. Compare the canyon walls on the right in this photograph with those in the previous photograph.

1750s. However, the village was the subject of frequent attacks by Comanches in 1760, and the residents fled north to Taos Pueblo for protection, remaining there until 1779. They then built a protective wall around the village, parts of which can still be seen today. The church was completed in 1815.

> It was a massive undertaking for Ranchos de Taos residents. One hundred thousand hand-formed adobe bricks were made. Thirty-two vigas, each at least 32 feet long, were cut to span the nave along with 28 vigas for the transept, each at least 25 feet long.[9]

Moving on from Ranchos, the Detourists came north into the town of Taos proper. In 1796, the Don Fernando de Taos land grant was awarded to Spanish settlers for the land south of Taos Pueblo, and they formed the town of Taos. The Detour drivers probably let the dudes off in Taos Plaza where they could wander there, and along Kit Carson Road to visit the home of frontiersman Kit Carson. Also on Kit Carson Road were the homes and galleries of Taos Society of Artist members E. I. Couse, J. H. Sharp, and Victor Higgins, whose paintings could be purchased at a fraction of the cost for which they sell today. Besides the Detourists, famous visitors to Taos of that era included Georgia O'Keefe, Ansel Adams, D. H. Lawrence, and Mabel Dodge Luhan.

The front of the beautiful San Francisco de Asis adobe church in Ranchos de Taos. Ranchos de Taos is approximately four miles south of Taos Plaza.

The back of the San Francisco de Asis church with its huge buttresses has always attracted artists and photographers including Georgia O'Keeffe and Ansel Adams.

The Indian Detours brochure showed this photograph of the Don Fernando Hotel in Taos where the Detourists had lunch and could choose whether to stay the night or head back to Santa Fe.

After lunch at the Don Fernando Hotel, the Detourists moved on north to Taos Pueblo, about three miles from town. Archeologists have dated the construction of Taos Pueblo at about 1350 A.D. The five-story adobe structure on the north bank of the Rio Pueblo is an astounding sight with Taos Mountain rising in the distance. The Couriers would tell of the history of the Pueblo—how it joined in the Pueblo Revolt of 1680 where seventy Spaniards were killed including two Franciscan priests, and how the Pueblo joined in the Taos revolt of 1847:

> On January 19, 1847, a group of Taos Pueblo Indians and Spanish settlers broke into the home of Charles Bent, the newly appointed American governor of the territory. Bent and several other Americans were killed in what became known as the Taos Revolt ... Finding most of the rebels holed up in the San Geronimo Church in Taos Pueblo, the U.S. army bombarded the church with cannon fire and destroyed it, killing most of the people inside. The rebellion was crushed.[10]

The Couriers would point out the remains of the church on the western edge of Taos Pueblo, and then let the dudes wander through the Pueblo, buying snacks and arts and crafts from the Natives. Many ceremonial dances were held at the Pueblo throughout the year, and historic photographs show hundreds of visitors sitting and standing on the walls of the Pueblo. This, of course, is no longer allowed.

After the Pueblo visit, the dudes were bused back to the Don Fernando Hotel for dinner and an overnight stay if they were on a two-day or longer Detour.

Edward Kemp took this photograph of Taos Pueblo c. 1927 with a Harveycar parked in the plaza, and Taos Pueblo Natives standing on top of the multi-storied pueblo. Snow-covered Taos Mountain rises in the background.

Taos Pueblo photographed in 1936 by Arthur Rothstein for the Farm Security Administration, with clothes hanging out to dry and bread baking ovens in the foreground. [*Library of Congress, LC-USF34-002901-D*]

The ruins of the San Geronimo mission church at Taos Pueblo in 1907. The church was destroyed by the U.S. Army in 1847 in response to the Taos Revolt which killed Charles Bent, the U.S. governor of New Mexico Territory. [*Phot. CL313(146), photograph by Carl Moon, Huntington Library*]

Left: Just north of Taos Pueblo this rider was heading back to the pueblo with El Salto Peak in the background to the left and Taos Mountain to the right. [*Phot. CL313(125), photograph by Carl Moon, 1907, Huntington Library*]

Below: Large crowds gathered at Taos Pueblo to watch the dances in the plaza below in the early 1900s. Ceremonials at Taos Pueblo still draw large crowds today, but visitors are no longer allowed on the buildings. [*Library of Congress, LC-USZ6-72458*]

5

Detours from Santa Fe: Land Cruises

The success of the Indian Detours and the Roads to Yesterday in 1926 spawned repeat tourist visits in 1927, and those tourists wanted to see more—more landscapes, more Indian ruins, more of everything that New Mexico, Arizona, and Southern Colorado had to offer. Fred Harvey was happy to oblige:

> The Santa Fe Transportation headquarters would gladly line out tours of any desired duration, provide the cars, arrange accommodations and meals, provide a personal courier and a capable driver … The fee was $65 a day for one, $70 a day for two, $25 a day per person for three to five people.[1]

Not all tourists were that independent though, and some desired a structured trip devised by Fred Harvey. To meet that demand, scenic "Motor Land Cruises" were devised. These would be longer trips of several days and several hundred miles. One of the first Land Cruises to be developed was the Sierra Verde Cruise, which began in July 1927. It was to cover 900 miles over eight days, taking in the Indian ruins in Northwestern New Mexico and Southwestern Colorado, along with the spectacular mountain ranges crossed on the way. The cruise would be offered only in the summer months because of the heavy winter snow in the mountains.

The Sierra Verde (Green Mountain) Cruise could begin in either Santa Fe or Albuquerque depending on where the tourist detrained. From Santa Fe a new motor route was devised which did not involve the trip over La Bajada Hill. Instead, the route went directly south from Santa Fe to the old mining towns of Cerillos (turquoise mines), and Madrid and Golden (gold mines). Farther south the road turned west across the southern edge of the Sandia Mountains and then on to Albuquerque for a night at the Alvarado Hotel. The next day, guests from the Alvarado joined the tour, which proceeded northwest to Chaco Canyon National Monument (now named Chaco Culture National Historical Park). Arriving at Chaco late afternoon, the dudes were given a Park Service Ranger-led tour of Pueblo Bonito, before bedding down for the night at Pueblo Bonito Lodge, "where rooms might not be luxurious, but they lived up to the Harvey rules of cleanliness and comfort."[2] This Pueblo Bonito Lodge was most likely in rooms at a nearby trading post.

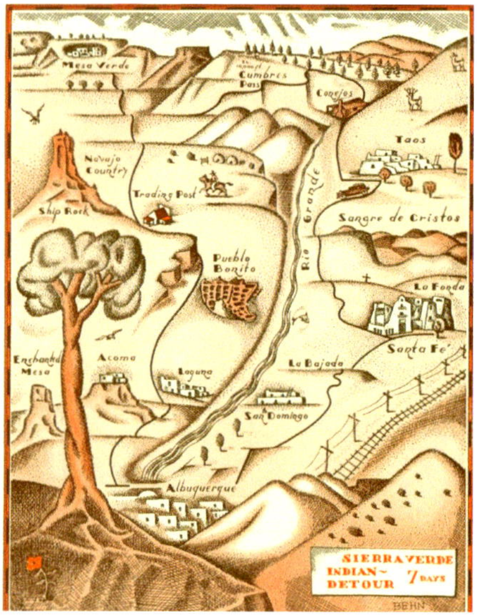

A highly stylized "map" of the Sierra Verde Land Cruise appeared in the 1930 Indian Detours brochure. The exaggerated map did show the general route from Santa Fe and Albuquerque to Chaco Canyon (Pueblo Bonito), Mesa Verde, Cumbres Pass, Conejos, and Taos.

> Chaco Canyon served as a major center of ancestral Puebloan culture (850–1150). Remarkable for its monumental buildings, distinctive architecture, astronomy, artistic achievements, it served as a hub of ceremony, trade, and administration for the Four Corners area—unlike anything before or since.[3]

Pueblo Bonito is the largest of the "great houses" at Chaco Canyon. "The name 'great house' is an apt description: the pueblo has more than 300 ground floor rooms and perhaps contained as many as 650 in all. The site rose to four or five stories in the back near the canyon wall."[4] Sixteen great houses are interpreted within the park, with several scattered along the nine-mile stretch of the canyon floor. Each great house had several kivas, which were round spiritual/ceremonial centers. Great kivas were quite large, holding up to 400 people. Smaller clan kivas could hold 50-100 people. After their relaxing night's sleep, the Detourists had the next morning to explore some of the other great houses in Chaco Canyon, before returning to their vehicles for an afternoon drive to Farmington and the night's lodging at the Avery Hotel.

The next morning the Detourists went to Aztec Ruins National Monument fourteen miles northeast of Farmington. Aztec is approximately sixty miles due north of Chaco and aerial photographs reveal a prehistoric road directly linking the two. Aztec is one of "a regional system of communities, centered in Chaco Canyon and linked by prehistoric road and trade networks throughout the San Juan Basin."[5]

After exploring the great kiva and pueblo at Aztec, the dudes headed north to Durango, Colorado, and then west to Mesa Verde National Park, another Ancestral Puebloan site. The Harveycars drove them twenty miles south of the park entrance to Chapin Mesa, where the dudes could explore the museum/visitor center and gaze down at the ruins of Spruce Tree House. This was their first introduction to the cliff houses of Mesa Verde. Ancestral Puebloan settlement had begun on the mesa tops where it was easier to grow crops, hunt game, and procure water. About 1200 A.D. they moved

Pueblo Bonito at Chaco Canyon as viewed from the cliffs above. The round circular areas were kivas, while residents lived in the square areas towards the back of the cliff. The large number of kivas signified Chaco's importance as a major religious/cultural center for the Ancestral Puebloans. [*Wikipedia Commons*]

An overhead view of Aztec Ruins National Monument shows several kivas and residences. The great kiva in the lower center was restored in 1934 by archaeologist Earl Morris. [*National Park Service*]

down into the curved openings in the cliffs below, possibly for protection from enemies, though no evidence of warfare has been found there. "By the mid-1200s these cliff dwellings housed about half the population of Chapin Mesa in ... Spruce Tree House, Cliff Palace, Balcony House, Long House, Mug House and others"[6] Around 1300 these dwellings were all abandoned, as drought apparently drove the residents out of Mesa Verde.

The Detourists spent the "night among the cedars in the jolly little log cabins of Spruce Tree Lodge."[7] The next morning, they had half a day to explore more ruins including Cliff Palace, the largest ruin in the park. Then it was back north out of the park and east a few miles to Mancos, where they spent the night at the Wrightsman Hotel, resting up for the spectacular mountain drive which would unfold on the sixth day.

The drive went from Mancos to Durango, east to Pagosa Springs, and then south into New Mexico to the mountain village of Chama, where the Denver & Rio Grande Railroad's narrow-gauge trains chugged in from Cumbres Pass. The highway followed the railroad line east over Cumbres Pass, descended to La Manga Pass, and then dropped into the Conejos River valley, where the dudes stayed the night at Barlow's Ranch. On the seventh day the tour continued east to Antonito, Colorado, and then north a bit before crossing the Rio Grande. Then the tour went south back into New Mexico through Carson National Forest and on to Taos, where there was time in the afternoon for a tour of the pueblo and artist studios. After an overnight stay at the Don Fernando Hotel, the brochure proclaimed that the last day of the Sierra Verde cruise "holds the Rio Grande gorges, luncheon under the Puye cliffs and La Fonda once more—after seven nights and seven full days a-roaming."[8]

Another Land Cruise developed in 1927 was the trip to Carlsbad Caverns in southeastern New Mexico. This four-day, 750-mile cruise was distinct from the Indian Detours in that it did not emphasize Indian ruins or living pueblos. Its focus was simply the big cave 25 miles south of Carlsbad, and the other sights were incidental along the way.

Leaving La Fonda in Santa Fe, the Harveycars proceeded southeast across the barren landscape to the small towns of Encino and Vaughn. The Los Chavez Harvey House was built in Vaughn in 1910, and the dudes probably stopped for lunch there, although the 1929 brochure stated, "lunch at Gran Quivira, Vaughn." That was puzzling since the Gran Quivira National Monument was ninety highway miles southwest of Vaughn and would not be visited until the return trip. The brochure writer must have got his facts mixed up.

> With only 11 guest rooms, Los Chavez was only slightly larger than Lamy's eight-room El Ortiz. Seldom housing overnight travelers, Los Chavez served as a dorm for local teachers; seven of its guest rooms were normally reserved for teachers who taught at the nearby public school.[9]

After lunch, the trip continued southeast from Vaughn to Roswell and then to Carlsbad, where the dudes spent the night at the Crawford Hotel. The next day, the Harveycars covered the 25 miles from Carlsbad to the "Carlsbad Cave National Monument." On the drive the Couriers told the dudes that President Calvin Coolidge designated the cave a National Monument on October 25, 1923. They explained that

Above left: Spruce Tree House is the first Ancestral Puebloan ruin visitors see from the visitor center/museum on Chapin Mesa at Mesa Verde National Park. (*National Park Service, 1930*)

Above right: Cliff Palace, the largest ruin at Mesa Verde, was photographed by J. Dixon on November 10, 1930. [*National Park Service*]

Above left: Herman Schweizer, head of Fred Harvey's Indian Department, sits near the Round Tower in Cliff Palace in 1931. Mary Colter also saw this tower, and it provided inspiration for her Desert View Watchtower at the Grand Canyon. [*National Park Service*]

Above right: The dudes, Couriers, and drivers take a break on the road over Cumbres Pass along the Colorado-New Mexico border in this view from the 1930 Indian Detours brochure.

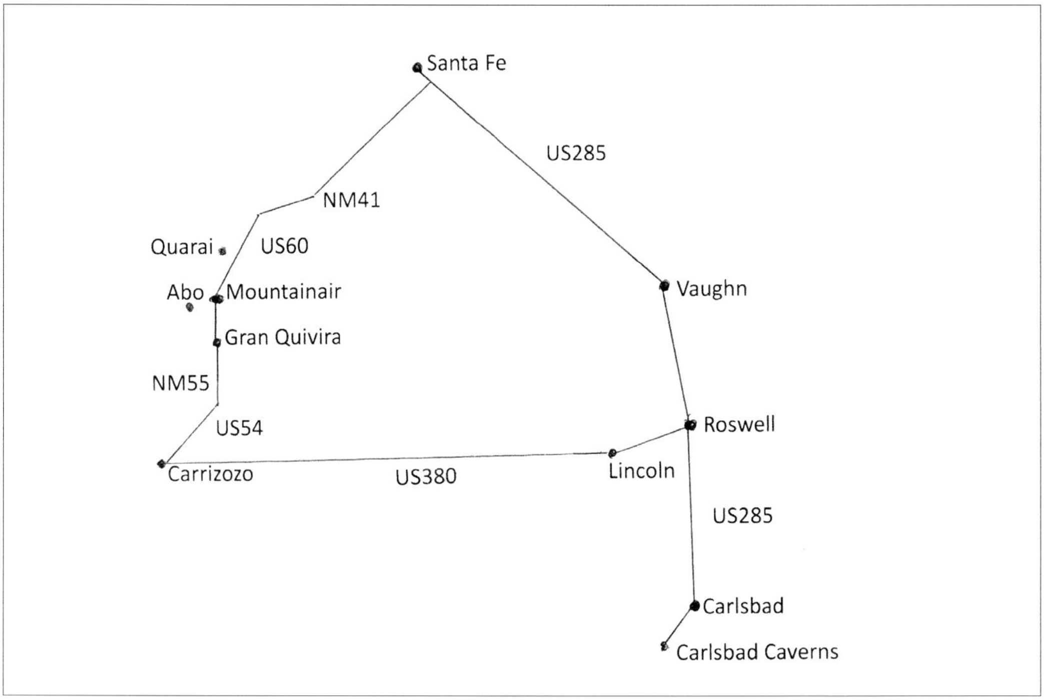

Schematic diagram of the route of the Land Cruise to Carlsbad Caverns from Santa Fe. The trip south went through Vaughn and Roswell to Carlsbad, while the return trip went west to Carrizozo and north to Mountainair. Today's highway numbers are shown.

Los Chavez Harvey House at Vaughn was built in 1910, and probably provided lunch for the Detourists on the trip south to Carlsbad.

a local cowboy, Jim White, had discovered the caves in the early 1900s when he saw "smoke" rising mysteriously from the plains. Investigating, he found that the smoke was actually a huge column of bats rising out of a hole in the ground. Creating a crude ladder, White descended underground and found a colossal cavern with colorful formations descending from the ceiling and rising from the ground. The Couriers explained to the dudes that stalactites descend from the ceiling, and stalagmites rise up from the ground. Sometimes the stalactites and stalagmites join together and form a column from the floor to the ceiling. White's discovery was highly publicized by the photographs of Ray V. Davis from 1916 to 1923 when National Monument status was granted.

> Within months, Dr. Willis T. Lee of the U.S. Geological Survey was investigating the cavern and was inspired to publish details of his visit in the January 1924 issue of National Geographic magazine. Later that same year, National Geographic bankrolled Lee to conduct an extended expedition into the cavern ... (which) elevated the cavern in the national consciousness. The public excitement generated by Lee's work stirred official interest in Washington, and on May 14, 1930, Congress designated the cave and surrounding land as Carlsbad Caverns National Park.[10]

When the Couriers and dudes entered the cave in 1927, they were guided by National Park Service Rangers. Conditions were still quite primitive. In 1924, National Park Service Director Stephen Mather and Willis Lee had descended into the cave in a miner's bucket attached to cables.

In 1924 National Park Service Director Stephen Mather (right) accompanied National Geographic photographer Willis T. Lee (left) on an exploration of Carlsbad Caverns. They were lowered into the cave in this mining bucket. It is difficult to believe that just three years later the Detourists walked into an entrance pathway to the cave. [*National Park Service*]

By 1927 a trail had been developed from the surface into the cave, so that the dudes could walk in "wearing stout walking shoes and warm sweaters."[11] With lanterns provided by the Rangers, the dudes walked in the cool 56 degree (F) steady temperature of the cave and marveled at the sight of the Big Room, which is approximately 4,000 feet long, 625 feet wide, and 255 feet high. The Couriers carried basket lunches for the dudes, and they were really ready for refreshment after their one-mile hike into the Big Room, and subsequent one-mile hike around the Big Room. Today, visitors can ride in an elevator from the Big Room back to the surface, but in 1927 the dudes had to hike back out to the cave entrance. After their day of exploring, they headed back to Carlsbad for another night at the Crawford Hotel.

The third day of the Carlsbad Cruise:

> the cars headed (northwest) toward Mountainair, going through Roswell to Lincoln, where the Couriers explained the confusing details of the Lincoln Country Cattle War of 1877. They poked around the jail where Billy the Kid was imprisoned in 1881 ... The Couriers talked about the volcanic lava flow of Carrizozo.[12]

From Carrizozo, the Harveycars headed north fifty miles to the Gran Quivira National Monument. There, the dudes finally got to see some Indian ruins on this tour. Today, Gran Quivira is part of the Salinas Pueblo Missions National Monument which was formed when two nearby New Mexico state monuments (Abo and Quarai) were added to Gran Quivira in the 1980s. The Visitor Center is in Mountainair, with Abo nine miles to the west, Quarai eight miles to the north, and Gran Quivira twenty-five miles to the south. All three sites share a similar history with Pueblo Indians settling there in the 1300s, and Franciscan Spanish priests constructing missions there from 1622 to 1635. Thus, the dudes saw the Pueblo ruins and the ruins of the churches at these sites. All the sites were abandoned by 1675 when drought and Apache attacks drove the Puebloans west to the Rio Grande valley. After visiting Gran Quivira, the dudes spent the night in Mountainair.

On the final day of the Carlsbad Cruise, the Harveycars headed north to Santa Fe, stopping at the Quarai ruins, and "quaint Mexican mountain villages when feasible" according to the 1929 brochure. It was only ninety miles from Quarai to Santa Fe, so the dudes were probably glad to escape the hot, dusty air of the deserts for the cool mountain air of Santa Fe and a relaxing night at La Fonda Hotel, before boarding their train the next day at Lamy.

In 1929, another Land Cruise was developed by extending the three-day Taos Indian Detour to four days. This was accomplished by adding the "Enchanted Circle" route north of Taos. This was "an exceptionally scenic 90-mile swing through the Cimarron and Red River canyons, the Mexican villages of Questa and Arroyo Hondo, the Carson National Forest and the upper Taos Valley."[13] Also in 1929, a Land Cruise was developed from Santa Fe to the Grand Canyon, covering five days. This Cruise will be discussed in Chapter 9, so that the design work of Mary Colter for the Fred Harvey Company can be discussed in greater detail.

In 1930, perhaps the strangest Land Cruise was developed. This involved Harveycars departing the train station in Raton, New Mexico, and heading 100 miles west to Taos. This was made possible by the completion of the paved road from Raton to

Right: This stalagmite in the Giant Dome room of Carlsbad Caverns was the largest discovered through 1934. It is sixteen feet in diameter and is estimated to be 60 million years old. [*National Park Service, photograph by George Grant, 1934*]

Below left: The dudes and their driver rest at the base of the giant stalagmite in Carlsbad Caverns shown in this photograph from the 1930 Indian Detours brochure.

Below right: The "Hall of Giants" in Carlsbad Caverns was photographed in 1941 by Ansel Adams for his Mural Project for the National Park Service. [*National Park Service*]

At the Gran Quivira site, which the Detourists visited on their way back from Carlsbad Caverns, the pueblo ruins are shown in the foreground and the ruins of the mission church in the background. [*Wikipedia Commons*]

Taos in 1930. The strange aspect was that the Harveycars had to be deadheaded from Santa Fe to the Raton train station at great expense to the Transportation Company. A "deadheading" surcharge was added to the fare for the dudes, but it did not fully cover the Company's expenses. This was a four-day cruise, with the first day from Raton through Cimarron Canyon to Eagle Nest Lake to Red River and on south to Taos. The route then followed the itinerary of the three-day Taos Indian Detour.

By March of 1931, the effects of the Great Depression were really affecting the Harvey Company's profits. As much as Harvey loved the Indian Detours, a decision was made to cut losses and sell the Transportation Company to its manager Hunter Clarkson. Clarkson changed the name of the company to Hunter Clarkson Tours, and the Harveycars became "Couriercars." The company logo was changed from the thunderbird to two entwined eagle dancers. The land cruises were cancelled, and three-day detours were run only from Santa Fe and Winslow, Arizona where the new La Posada Harvey Hotel had opened in 1930. Oddly enough, the Harvey Company kept its Harveycars in operation at the Grand Canyon since operations there, in conjunction with its El Tovar Hotel, continued to be profitable. To protect these profits, Couriercars were not allowed to run at the Grand Canyon. They had to deposit their dudes at El Tovar, and then the dudes transferred to Harveycars.

6

Detours from Albuquerque

During the glory years before the Great Depression, the Harvey Company ran a few Indian Detours from Albuquerque starting in 1926. "Some of the tours were suggested as possible fill-ins for people with a half-day between trains after or before completing the Detours; others were long enough to require the tourist to spend extra days in Albuquerque."[1] One popular half-day Detour was the three-hour round trip to the west side of Albuquerque to see the three extinct volcanoes (named Vulcan, Black, and JA—for nearby St. Joseph Academy). Today these extinct volcanoes are incorporated in Petroglyph National Monument, which was created on June 27, 1990, and includes three canyons to the northeast of the volcanoes where thousands of petroglyphs were incised on the black rock by Native Americans and early Spanish settlers.

One-day trips from Albuquerque went northwest to Jemez Pueblo, and west to Laguna and Acoma Pueblos. The sixty-mile trip out to Jemez Pueblo bypassed Zia Pueblo:

> This pueblo was not for visiting. For despite the friendly relationship between the majority of the Indians and the Harvey organization, a few, like the Zias, resented outsiders and were not only unfriendly but in some cases hostile.[2]

Jemez people migrated from the Mesa Verde area in the 1300s and built several pueblos in the Jemez River valley. They participated in the Pueblo Revolt of 1680, and upon the Spanish reconquest in 1692, they were forced to consolidate at the one pueblo in today's location. "The Jemez Reservation covers 90,000 acres, but does not include the prehistoric pueblo sites, which are located on national forest lands."[3] One of those prehistoric pueblo sites is Giusewa Pueblo, which is located twelve miles north of Jemez Pueblo at Jemez Springs. The Detourists visited here and saw the remains of the pueblo and the Franciscan mission church San Jose de los Jemez. The church was built in 1621-22. This site was abandoned after the Pueblo Revolt. If the Detourists "wanted to bathe in the hot springs and not rush back to Albuquerque, the trip could be extended to allow an overnight stay at La Esperanza Hotel in Jemez Springs."[4]

Another day trip from Albuquerque took the dudes sixty miles west to Laguna and Acoma Pueblos. The tour took the Detourists first to Acoma and then backtracked to

Jemez Pueblo stretches out along the Jemez River seen in the background with cattle grazing in the foreground. This is the site where several scattered pueblos were consolidated after the Spanish reconquest of 1692. (*Photograph by W. Brown, 1890, Phot. CL215(9), Huntington Library*]

The remains of the Franciscan mission church San Jose de los Jemez which is twelve miles north of Jemez Pueblo at Jemez Springs. It is now a state historic site. [*Photograph by W. Brown, 1890, Phot. CL215(16), Huntington Library*]

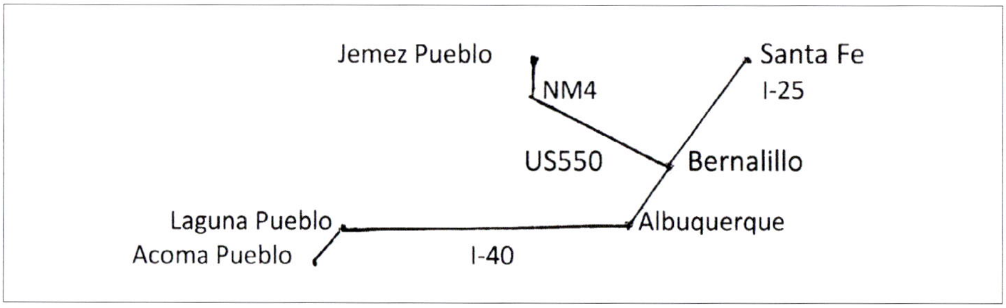

A schematic diagram of the Indian Detour from Santa Fe and Albuquerque to Jemez Pueblo, Laguna Pueblo, and Acoma Pueblo, with today's highway numbers shown.

Laguna, where the dudes could either stay overnight or proceed back to Albuquerque. Acoma Pueblo is located on top of a 376-foot-high sandstone butte and is appropriately known as "Sky City." Settlement in two-and-three story adobe buildings on top of the butte occurred between 950–1150 A.D. "Until the early twentieth century, Acoma remained accessible only by a rough foot trail, and the residents of the impregnable mesa-top community fiercely resisted acculturation."[5] The residents also fiercely resisted Spanish intrusion and participated in the Pueblo Revolt of 1680, destroying the Spanish mission church. The mission church San Esteban Rey was constructed in 1699 on top of the remains of the original church. In 1926, when the Detourists visited Acoma, they ascended the old trail to the mesa top and visited the church. Visitors today have the option of using the trail or riding the shuttle bus to the top on a road constructed in the 1940s when Hollywood filmmakers came to shoot a movie. Very few people live year-round in Sky City today as there is no running water or electricity. However, many do live in the pueblo homes during ceremonies and feast days. Acoma today welcomes visitors and is well known for its beautiful white pottery.

Laguna Pueblo, just to the east of Acoma, is unique of all the New Mexican pueblos in that it is the only one constructed after the Pueblo Revolt of 1680. Following the Spanish reconquest of 1692, residents of Cochiti and Santo Domingo Pueblos fled west and established a new pueblo here along the Rio San Jose. Spanish influence remained strong though, and a mission church, San Jose de la Laguna, was built at the pueblo from 1699–1701. The church still stands and was visited by the Detourists in 1926.

The terraced homes at Acoma Pueblo were photographed by Ansel Adams in 1941. [*National Archives 519831*]

The mission church San Esteban Rey at Acoma Pueblo was photographed by Ansel Adams in 1941. At the time there was only a footpath to the top of the mesa as the road was not constructed until a few years later. [*National Archives, 519833*]

The Harvest Dance at Acoma Pueblo c. 1910. Notice the elaborate tablitas on the heads of the women dancers. [*Photograph by Carl Moon, Phot. CL313(233), Huntington Library*]

Timber for the viga beams in the church and the pueblo homes was hauled in from the forests along the slopes of 11,301-foot-high Mount Taylor, thirty miles to the north.

> In the 1880s, the Santa Fe Railway extended its tracks across the reservation, following the natural east-west travel corridor along the Rio San Jose ... Pueblo artists and craftsmen were able to sell their goods directly to tourist train passengers during brief rest stops.[6]

And of course, the Laguna artists would attempt to sell their goods to the Detourists when they visited.

The Laguna Reservation today is quite large, consisting of some 500,000 acres and six villages, located north and south of Interstate 40.

In 1929, a unique one-day Detour was created from Albuquerque to the top of Sandia Peak after the road was completed in 1928. This loop tour lasted 6 to 7 hours and was very scenic. From Albuquerque the tour proceeded east to Tijeras Canyon, then north through Tejano Canyon, and then west to the top of Sandia Peak, where a basket lunch was served to the dudes. After lunch, the drive descended a gravel road north to Placitas, west to Bernalillo, and south back to Albuquerque. This loop can be driven today after spring snow melt, but the author found the gravel road section to be extremely rough and was glad to have a high-clearance four-wheel-drive vehicle. Perhaps this section was in better shape in 1929.

An AT&SF train cuts through Laguna Pueblo in the early 1900s. The trains would usually stop there for a few minutes to give the pueblo residents an opportunity to sell their arts and crafts. [*Fred Harvey booklet, The Great Southwest, 1911*]

Laguna Pueblo with the mission church San Jose de la Laguna seen with the curving rooftop at the skyline to the left. [*Photograph by Carl Moon, circa 1904, Phot. CL313(253), Huntington Library*]

A closeup of the San Jose de la Laguna Church today with a horno oven in the foreground.

A spectacular view of Albuquerque from the top of Sandia Peak was seen by the Detourists when the Sandia Peak loop tour was established in1929. A paved road leads to a parking area at the top today.

The Carlsbad Canyon Land Cruise had also been offered from Albuquerque as well as Santa Fe; however, as the Great Depression deepened in the 1930s, this option was dropped. By 1932, all Detours from Albuquerque had ceased. To give the cross-country train traveler a taste of the New Mexican pueblos, a hurry-up trip to Isleta Pueblo south of Albuquerque was arranged. The Santa Fe Railway's brochure explained:

> Perhaps you are racing cross-continent on the Santa Fe's Grand Canyon Limited—without time to spare for a real New Mexico stopover. Even so, if you like, you can step off the train for forty minutes of motoring, leg-stretching and sight-seeing in New Mexico's crisp, bracing air, without the slightest inconvenience or the loss of a moment in reaching your destination. Here is how it may be done ... [7]

For one dollar, the eastbound train passenger could depart at Isleta station, take fifteen minutes to walk about the church and pueblo, then board a Harveycar for a quick ride north to Albuquerque, where they would rejoin the train which had stopped at the depot for a twenty-minute break. Westbound passengers could depart the train at Albuquerque, hop on a Harveycar to Isleta, walk about, and then reboard the train at the Isleta station. This was what the once grand Indian Detours from Albuquerque had been reduced to during the height of the Great Depression.

7

Detours from Gallup

As the Indian Detours grew in popularity in the years before the Great Depression, Fred Harvey began to offer Detours from Gallup in Northwest New Mexico, where the AT & SF Railway had established the town in 1881. Fred Harvey's El Navajo Hotel was built in Gallup in 1923, and in 1929 served as an outpost for a series of Detours. This proved popular with tourists since they could detrain at Gallup and board Harveycars from El Navajo, rather than having to ride Harveycars all the way out west from Santa Fe or Albuquerque.

Gallup was named after David L. Gallup, who was a paymaster for the AT&SF. "On payday railroad workers would announce they were 'going to Gallup's' to collect their money."[1] Gallup was located just outside the eastern boundary of the Navajo Reservation and was:

> the main shipping point and buying center for the Navajo wool clip, thousands of pounds being shipped annually … and the shipping of sheep and cattle from the grazing lands of the Zuni mountains are important activities here. The town serves as a trading point for the Zuni and Navajo from the near-by reservations.[2]

Gallup made a convenient departure point for Detours to the Zuni, Navajo, and Hopi reservations and the magnificent canyons and mesas of the area.

Zuni Pueblo was thirty miles south of Gallup and was the first stop on a one-day Detour which also included El Morro National Monument with Inscription Rock, and the Bandera ice caves and lava flows. Zuni Reservation today has approximately 450,000 acres and 19,000 residents. It is unique from the other New Mexican pueblos in that it has its own language. Today:

> Zuni artisans produce more fine traditional Pueblo art and craft items than their counterparts at any other pueblo. Perhaps 75 percent of the Zuni populace makes a living from some form of art … particularly … Zuni silver jewelry and carved stone animal fetishes.[3]

The Zuni area was settled perhaps as early as 750 A.D. when pit houses were developed. When Spanish explorer Coronado visited the pueblo in 1540, he found multi-storied

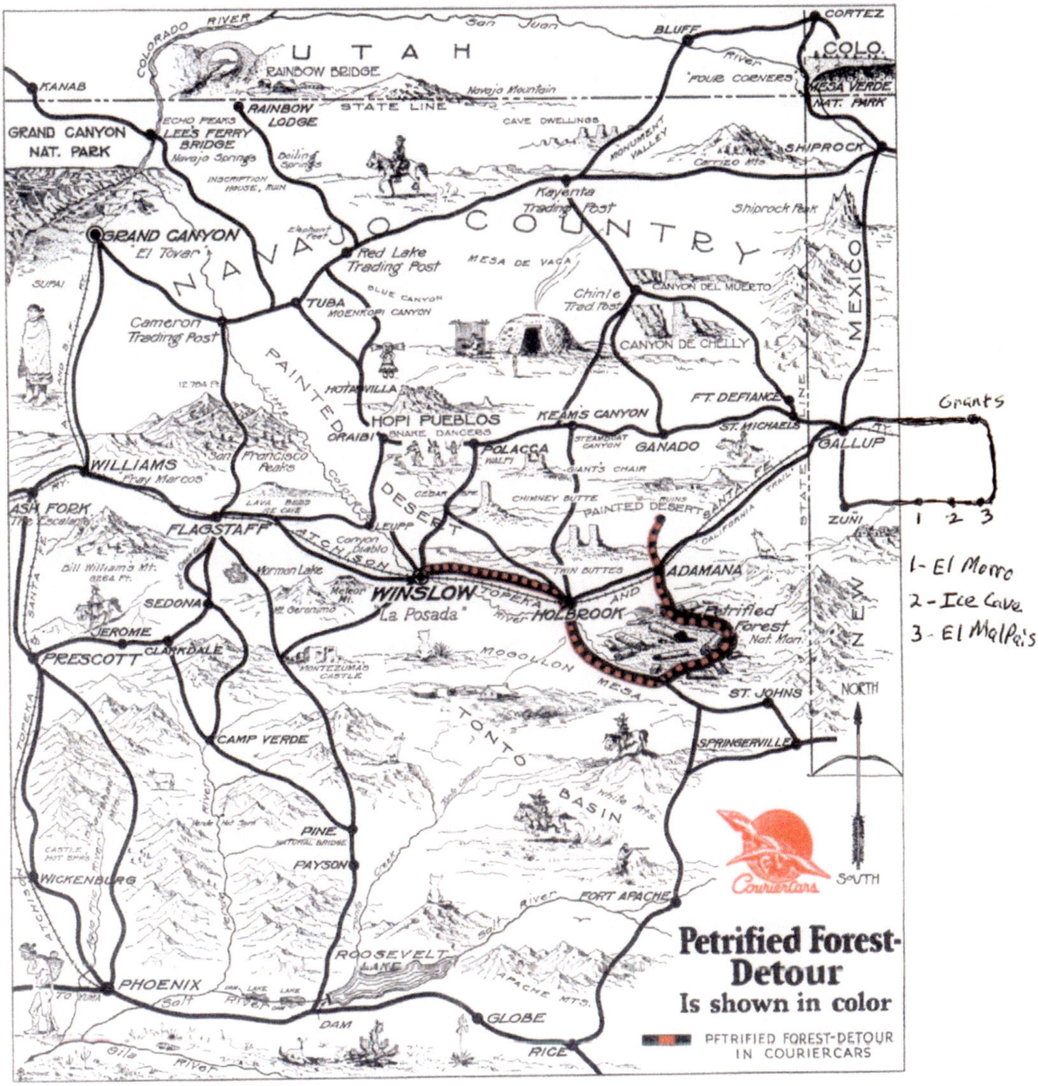

The Indian Detours brochure of 1938 included this detailed map of Detours in Arizona from Winslow. Gallup, New Mexico was also shown on the map, and the author added the Detour from Gallup to Zuni, El Morro, Ice Cave, and El Malpais to the map.

houses of adobe bricks, not the seven cities of gold he was expecting. Zuni had six villages scattered around the mesas, but no gold. Zuni participated in the Pueblo Revolt of 1680, despite the language difference from their fellow pueblos. They submitted to the Spanish reconquest in 1692, and returned to growing beans, corn, and squash, and raising cattle and sheep. As water supplies grew increasingly scarce, the pueblo turned to arts and crafts for economic support, and the Detourists undoubtedly purchased some fine silver jewelry from them.

Next stop on the Detour was El Morro National Monument, twenty-five miles east of Zuni. This National Monument was established on December 8, 1906, by President Theodore Roosevelt. *El Morro* is Spanish for "the headland" and the monument is home to Inscription Rock, a large sandstone bluff located on the old trade route between Zuni and Acoma Pueblos. It has a pool of water at its base which has always attracted travelers passing through this barren desert landscape. The travelers would inscribe their names on the rock as they passed through. One of the earliest inscriptions was by Juan de Oñate, Spanish governor of New Mexico, on the 16th of April 1605. The Detourists probably did not have time to hike the trail to the top of the bluff where there are the ruins of an Anasazi village inhabited from 1275 to 1350 A.D. which had approximately 355 rooms and a population of 600.

Motoring on east another fourteen miles, the Detourists stopped to explore the Bandera Volcano Ice Cave. This cave is a lava tube containing permanent ice in its year-round temperature of 31 degrees Fahrenheit. The ice was harvested by Indians and other travelers along the route. The lava tube was formed during the Bandera Crater eruption 9,500–10,900 years ago.

> A lava tube is formed when molten lava pours out of a volcano. The surface hardens, while below, the lava continues to flow. This creates a pipeline of lava known as a lava tube. This is the Bandera lava tube. Its overall length is 17.5 miles and is considered to be the longest in North America. Most of the lava tube has collapsed ... (leaving) caves here and there.[4]

In the 1930s, after the Detours, a trading post was established at the Ice Cave, trails were developed, and admission was charged. Removal of ice from the cave was stopped in 1946. The attraction is still open to travelers today.

The Ice Cave is at the western edge of a huge flow of black hardened lava which imposed an impenetrable barrier to east-west travel for the Pueblo Indians and the Spanish. Travelers had to skirt its northern edge, as did the route of the Detourists (today it's New Mexico State Road 53). As the Detourists passed by, they marveled at the lava flows, cinder cones, lava tubes, and caves, all part of the Zuni-Bandera volcanic field created by a series of eruptions over the past 60,000 years. The area was finally protected in 1987 by President Ronald Reagan who designated 114, 276 acres as El Malpais National Monument. *El Malpais* is what the Spanish had called the lava fields—"the bad country."

From there, the Detour proceeded twenty-five miles north to Grants, and then sixty miles west back to Gallup for a relaxing night at El Navajo Hotel and a fine Fred Harvey meal.

This view of Zuni Pueblo was photographed by John Hillers in 1880 showing the stone homes with flat roofs and chimneys. The view is southeast toward Corn Mountain. [*Phot. CL 190(17), Huntington Library*]

The Zuni Mission Church, Nuestra Señora de Guadalupe, today is closed, and the Pueblo is seeking funds for its restoration.

Photographer Alexander Gardner may have accompanied the survey crew of the Kansas Pacific Railroad (precursor of the AT&SF) in 1868 when he photographed Inscription Rock at El Morro.

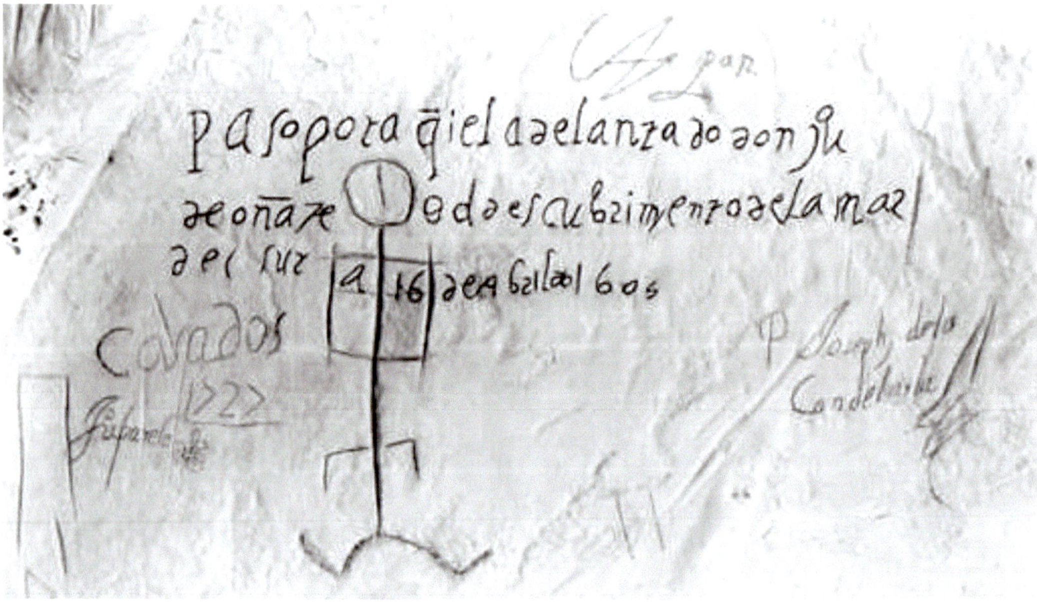

Inscriptions on the rock at El Morro date back as far as 1605, when Spanish governor Don Juan de Oñate carved his name and date into the rock. [*Photograph by George Grant, 1934, National Park Service*]

The Bandera Volcano Ice Cave still attracts a large number of visitors today to its cool depths.

Hardened layers of lava from the Bandera Volcano eruption are seen at El Malpais National Monument. [*U.S. Geological Survey*]

By far the most popular Detour from Gallup was the journey to Canyon de Chelly, approximately ninety miles to the northwest. Indian Detours founder Hunter Clarkson played a major role in proposing the establishment of Canyon de Chelly as a National Monument. Clarkson recognized the value of preserving the beautiful canyons and Anasazi (Ancestral Puebloan) ruins which were threatened with erosion and vandalism, and he probably had in mind a future Detour there.

> In 1923 Hunter Clarkson, who operated transportation services in the Southwest in cooperation with the Santa Fe Railway, wrote Assistant Director of the National Park Service Arno B. Cammerer concerning such a proposal. Clarkson had previously discussed that matter with National Park Service Director Stephen T. Mather.[5]

It was not until April 1, 1931, however, that President Herbert Hoover declared Canyon de Chelly a national monument. The delay was caused by protracted negotiations with the Navajo tribe on whose land the Canyon was located. Finally, in 1931, the Navajo tribal council:

> unanimously agreed to accept the establishment of a national monument at Canyon de Chelly "providing the grazing and other rights of the Indians are in no way interfered with," and the Indians around Chinle wanted the exclusive right to furnish horses for the tourists.[6]

Those conditions still apply today, as approximately forty Navajo families live in the canyon raising corn and grazing sheep and cattle. The Navajo still retain the rights to taking tourists into the canyons, and jeep tours and hiking tours must be arranged with Navajo guides. The only trail open occasionally for tourists to hike into Canyon de Chelly without Navajo guides is the trail to the White House Anasazi ruins, which is about a two-hour round-trip hike. "The Canyon de Chelly Anasazi eventually deserted the area and settled on or around the Hopi mesas to the west, in the Zuni area, and along the Rio Grande."[7]

On the way to Canyon de Chelly in 1929, the Detourists undoubtedly stopped at the Hubbell Trading post one mile west of Ganado, Arizona. The Trading Post had been established by John Lorenzo Hubbell in 1878 to provide goods to the Navajo Nation in return for Navajo crafts, especially blankets. The Trading Post still exists today as the Hubbell Trading Post National Historic Site, established on August 28, 1965, and administered by the nonprofit Western National Parks Association.

When the Detourists visited Canyon de Chelly in 1929, they could explore three main canyons, each extending approximately twenty miles from west to east—Canyon de Chelly, Black Rock Canyon, and Canyon del Muerto, all of which are in the National Monument today. The trip could be two or three days long, depending on whether the Detourists wanted to take horseback rides into the canyons. The 1929 ATSF/Harvey brochure detailed the options available:

> With an early start from El Navajo Hotel, it is possible to reach McSparron's Ranch, where comfortable accommodations and good horses are available, during the afternoon. When no trail trip is made into the canyons, return to Gallup by motor is

Ansel Adams took this sweeping view of Canyon de Chelly in 1941. What looks like a large riverbed is actually a dry wash scoured wide when occasional downpours of rain occur. [*National Park Service*]

Above left: Frederick Monsen photographed the tall rock spires of Canyon de Chelly, c. 1900. [*Phot. CL312(18), Huntington Library*]

Above right: Edward S. Curtis photographed seven Navajo riders at the bottom of Canyon de Chelly in 1904. When the Detourists visited Canyon de Chelly, they had the opportunity to ride horses into the canyon. [*Library of Congress, LC-USZC4-11256*]

Left: Visitors at the White House ruins at Canyon de Chelly. The ruins are in the cave above as well as the ledge below. [*Indian Detours Brochure*]

Below: Charles Pierce photographed this Navajo family living among Anasazi ruins in the cliffs of Canyon de Chelly, c. 1910. [*Phot. CL Pierce 01683, Huntington Library*]

The Hubbell Trading Post in Ganado, Arizona, appears much the same today as it did when it was established in 1878. Now it is a National Historic Site, still serving as a trading post for the Navajo Nation and visiting tourists.

> made the second day. The supreme interest of this particular Cruise, however, lies in devoting the second day, and often the second night as well, to a leisurely exploration on horseback of points accessible in no other way, with return to El Navajo left for the third day.[8]

Today, Canyon de Chelly National Monument consists of about 84,000 acres located entirely within the Navajo Reservation. Lodging is available at the Navajo-owned Thunderbird Hotel between Chinle and the park boundary. "The National Park service and the Navajo Nation share resources and continue to work in partnership to manage this special place."[9]

Other Detours from Gallup in 1929 included trips to Chaco Canyon, Petrified Forest in Arizona, and the Hopi villages, which will be covered in the next chapter, since all Detours from Gallup were ceased in 1930 when Fred Harvey opened La Posada Hotel in Winslow, Arizona. That would be the base for future Detours to Hopi, Petrified Forest, Canyon de Chelly, Rainbow Bridge, and Monument Valley.

8

Detours from Winslow

Opening in May of 1930, La Posada Hotel in Winslow, Arizona, offered Fred Harvey guests seventy-five hotel rooms, fine dining, and a more convenient departure point than Gallup for the Arizona Detours. For the tourist with only one day for a Detour, a trip was offered from La Posada east to Petrified Forest in the morning, returning to La Posada for lunch, and then going west to Meteor Crater in the afternoon, before returning to La Posada in the evening. Longer tours from Winslow included trips to the Hopi villages, Canyon de Chelly, Rainbow Bridge, Monument Valley, and the Four Corners

Petrified Forest is about fifty-five miles east of Winslow. President Theodore Roosevelt designated the area as a national monument on December 8, 1906. It initially consisted of just the petrified forest area south of today's Interstate 40. In 1932, the Painted Desert section (north of today's Interstate 40) was added to the monument. In 1962, the entire area was designated as Petrified Forest National Park. The Detourists' trip there in 1930 probably stopped at the Painted Desert Inn in the northern section as well as the Petrified Forest in the southern section. The Inn was constructed in the 1920s by local businessman Herbert Lore. It was purchased by the National Park Service in 1935 and was remodeled by the Civilian Conservation Corps beginning in 1938. It was reopened in 1940 offering food, lodging, and souvenirs. It closed during World War II and reopened again under Fred Harvey management in 1947. Mary Colter redesigned the interior and Harvey Girls served guests in the dining room. The Inn closed in 1963, and after restoration in 2006, the Painted Desert Inn reopened as a museum within Petrified Forest National Park. (Photographs of Painted Desert Inn are included in Chapter 9). The dudes on the 1930 Detour witnessed the colorful hills in the Painted Desert section and then moved on south to view the Petrified Forest. "In the Petrified Forest most of the logs have been replaced at least in part by mineral matter, especially varieties of quartz, and they now contain little of the original organic matter."[1] Thus they were "petrified"—turned to stone. The petrified logs are from a conifer forest that grew in the area about 225 million years ago. The trees were 80 to 100 feet tall, and 3 to 4 feet in diameter, with some as tall as 200 feet and 10 feet in diameter at the base. Undoubtedly the dudes gasped when they saw these huge, petrified logs, and when the

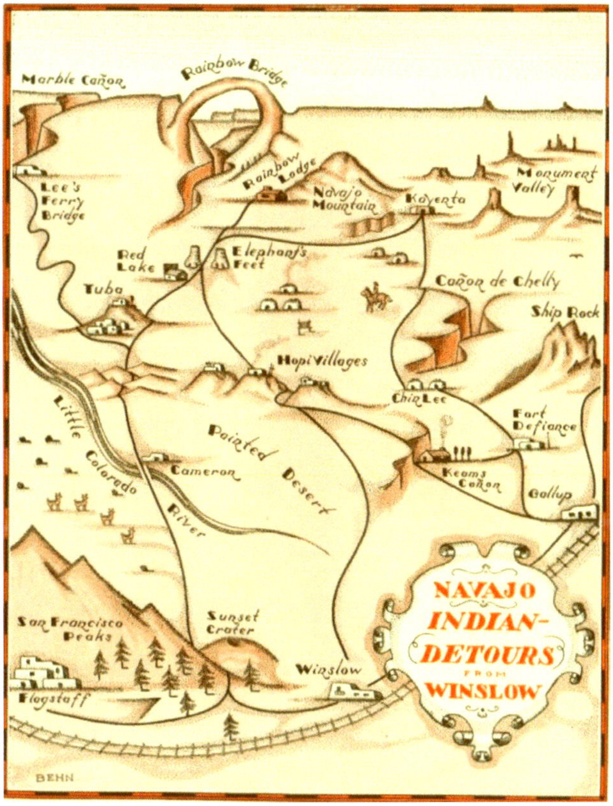

Right: This illustration from the 1930 Indian Detours brochure shows the major destinations for Detours from Winslow, including the Hopi villages, Canyon de Chelly, Rainbow Bridge, and Monument Valley.

Below: Finishing touches of construction were being completed in 1930 at La Posada Hotel in Winslow. The AT&SF train tracks right in front of the hotel offered a convenient departure point for passengers heading for the Arizona Indian Detours. [*Kansas Historical Society*]

Above left: Southwest ornamentations decorated the new Fred Harvey La Posada Hotel, as illustrated in this advertising brochure.

Above right: La Posada designed by Mary Colter and opened in 1930, provided an oasis in the desert for travelers. Restoration of the hotel began in 1997 by Allan Affeldt.

Above left: A Harveycoach prepares to leave La Posada for an Indian Detour in the 1930s. [*Photograph in Winslow Arts Trust Museum*]

Above right: The AT&SF station in Winslow has been restored and now houses the Affeldt Mion Museum (formerly the Winslow Arts Trust Museum).

Courier explained that "a cubic foot of petrified wood weighs about 168 pounds and has a hardness of about 7 on a scale of hardness from 1 to 10."[2]

After lunch back at La Posada, the Detour continued west eighteen miles to Meteor Crater. This has always been a privately owned site which charges admission ($27 for adults in 2023). The site is awesome though, and the dudes were favorably impressed. The crater was formed when a meteorite slammed into the earth about 50,000 years ago and created a depression that is 4,150 feet across and 570 feet deep. Most of the meteor vaporized upon impact. After viewing the crater, the dudes returned to La Posada for the night to board the train the next day or continue more Detours in Arizona.

Probably the most popular Detour from Winslow was the trip to the Hopi villages sixty miles due north. The Hopi villages were originally settled by Anasazi (Ancestral Puebloans) fleeing from the Four Corners area and from Canyon de Chelly in the late 1300s. "Because early (Spanish) explorers entered the Hopi villages from the east, the mesa sitting on the southernmost tip of Black Mesa became First Mesa, with Second Mesa and Third Mesa following."[3] These high mesas were easily defended against enemies. Each mesa contains three Hopi villages: First Mesa has the villages of Hano, Sichomovi, and Walpi; Second Mesa has the villages of Mishongovi, Shipalovi, and Shungopovi; Third Mesa has the villages of Oraibi, Hotevilla, and Bacavi. The Snake Dance at Walpi on First Mesa became the most famous for tourists to visit.

The Snake Dance ceremony was held in August. Hundreds of people came to witness what the ATSF/Harvey brochure called "the most extraordinary of American aboriginal ceremonials and is always accessible through a series of special Harveycar Motor Cruises."[4] The problem was that there was no lodging for the dudes in the Hopi villages. No problem—Fred Harvey simply set up their own village nearby. Accommodations:

> were loaded on trucks and brought to the site. Large tents complete with cots, blankets, pillows, lanterns, and wash basins made portable hotels, not up to the Harvey standards, but this was acceptable to the dudes. Tables and chairs were trucked out to make portable dining halls. Foodstuffs, beverages, cooking equipment, cooling devices, all assured the tourist they would eat unspoiled food, prepared in the Harvey (tradition).[5]

Erna Fergusson, the Courier trainer and handbook writer, described the Snake Dance in detail in her book *Dancing Gods: Indian Ceremonials of New Mexico & Arizona*, and readers are referred to the details there as they are quite long and complicated. She summed up the attraction thusly:

> Of all the Southwestern Indian ceremonials the Hopi Snake-dance attracts the most shivering attention. Everyone wants to see it, and every year more white visitors crowd the villages, threatening the frail roofs, making crude and loud comment, squirming in an agony of pleasant horror to see men handle venomous snakes ... Undoubtedly the Snake-dance is the most ancient ceremony we still may see, for it is the direct worship of the clan ancestor, who is the snake.[6]

To the Hopi, snakes were the original guardians of springs of water, so the dance was held in August to bring rain to their crops.

Above left: The Painted Desert lives up to its name with its various hues of red, gray, and green.

Above right: The size of some of the petrified logs in Petrified Forest National Park is illustrated by the two men in the photograph. [*Photograph by W. Brown, c. 1890, Phot. CL215(21), Huntington Library*]

Albert Einstein and his wife visited the Petrified Forest in 1931. Notice the petrified logs scattered on the hillside in the background. [*National Park Service*]

The Meteor Crater west of Winslow was an attraction for the Detourists after lunch at La Posada. Standing on the rim, the dudes would be 570 feet above the bottom of the crater. [*U.S. Geological Survey*]

Above left: The Hopi village of Walpi was photographed by Ansel Adams in 1941. The ruggedness of the terrain is readily apparent. [*National Park Service*]

Above right: Carl Moon photographed this street scene in Walpi, c. 1910. Notice the weaving loom on the second terrace of the dwellings. [*Phot. CL313(16), Huntington Library*]

Above left: The Hopi Snake Dances always attracted large crowds of visitors as witnessed by all the people on the rooftops at Shipaulovi. [*Photograph by Carl Moon, c. 1910, Phot. CL313(41), Huntington Library*]

Above right: A snake dangles from the mouth of a Hopi Dancer in this scene photographed by Carl Moon, c. 1910. [*Phot. CL313(20), Huntington Library*]

Today, Hopi dances:

> are no longer always open to non-Hopis. For years ... tour companies have brought tourists by the hundreds to view the ceremonies. But the villages and ancient rooftops were not designed to handle large crowds. More seriously, visitors have violated the Hopis' rules about not photographing or videotaping anything in the villages. This has resulted in the posting of "closed" signs at the road entrance during a dance.[7]

Like their relatives in New Mexico, the Hopi were not fond of the Spanish invasion and the Catholic Church. They joined in the Pueblo Revolt of 1680, and due to their isolation, they were not revisited by the Spanish until 1701, nine years after the Spanish Reconquest of the New Mexico pueblos in 1692.

The Hopi have always been farmers growing corn, beans, squash, melons, and other crops. Rain is essential for the crops in this harsh desert land. "Katsinas, or kachinas, as they are popularly called, are the very important spirit beings in Hopi cosmology who assure rain for the Hopis ... The Katsinas visit the Hopis and bring gifts."[8] Besides farming, the Hopi are craftsmen. "Hopi artisans are internationally recognized for their pottery, basketry, weaving, Katsina doll carving, and silversmithing."[9]

Nampeyo was a famous Hopi potter in the early 1900s, and Fred Harvey brought her to Hopi House at the Grand Canyon to demonstrate pottery making. Her descendants continue making pottery to this day. The Detourists undoubtedly saw and purchased some of these Hopi pots during their visits.

The 1930 ATSF/Harvey brochure illustrated Navajo Indian Detours from Winslow. Pictured were Canyon de Chelly (which previously had been visited from Gallup),

Nampeyo demonstrated her pottery technique for Carl Moon at a Hopi village. Fred Harvey brought Nampeyo to Hopi House at the Grand Canyon to demonstrate her pottery making. [*Photograph by Carl Moon, c. 1910, Phot. CL313(38), Huntington Library*]

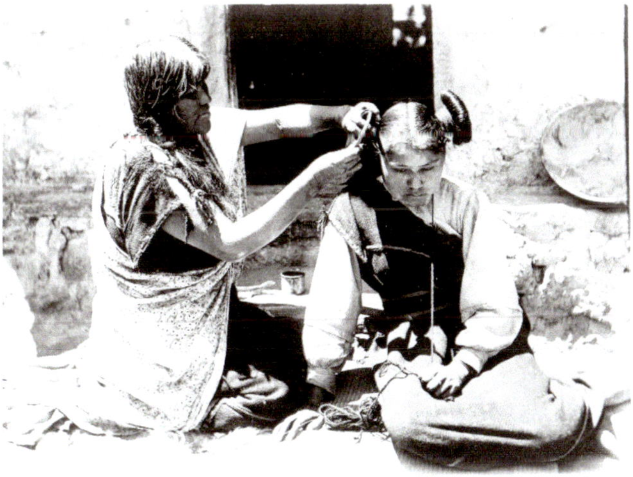

Above left: A Hopi maiden is having her hair styled in the traditional coiled "butterfly wing" fashion. This indicated her eligibility for marriage. [*Library of Congress, LC-USZ-1768*]

Above right: This is the finished product of the hairstyling for Hopi Maidens. [*Photograph by Carl Moon, c. 1910, Phot. CL313(10), Huntington Library*]

Rainbow Bridge, and Monument Valley. These were longer trips for intrepid travelers. Rainbow Bridge was 210 miles from Winslow and required an overnight stay at Rainbow Lodge. From there the dudes mounted horses the next day for the thirteen-mile ride to view Rainbow Bridge. The dudes camped there overnight, and the following day rode the thirteen miles back to Rainbow Lodge—definitely a trip for horse lovers.

The Ancestral Puebloans and local Native tribes had known of Rainbow Bridge for hundreds of years. They regarded it as a sacred religious place. White men had heard of this spectacular natural arch but had been unable to find it until a Paiute guide led a survey party there on August 14, 1909. The arch is so magnificent that it did not even take a year to proclaim it as a national monument, with President William Howard Taft making that declaration on May 30, 1910, to "preserve this extraordinary natural bridge, having an arch which is in form and appearance much like a rainbow."[10] Rainbow Bridge is one of the largest natural arches in the world. It is 290 feet from the base to the top of the arch, with a length of 275 feet. The top of the arch is 42 feet thick and 33 feet wide. This awesome sight rewarded the dudes at the end of their hot, dusty horseback ride. It's much easier for tourists to get there today, with a boat ride across Lake Powell and a 1.5-mile hike from the boat dock. However, with low water levels on the lake in 2023, the National Park Service advises visitors to "beach your boat and walk through muck to the trail at your own risk." Of course, Lake Powell did not exist at the time of the Detours. The Glen Canyon Dam on the Colorado River was approved in 1956 and construction was completed by 1963 when the gates on the dam were closed and waters started rising to form the lake.

Another natural phenomenon for the Detourists to explore in Northern Arizona was the sandstone spires and buttes of Monument Valley, approximately 100 miles east of Rainbow Bridge. Monument Valley stretches from Kayenta, Arizona, to Mexican Hat, Utah. The most famous landmarks are now preserved in the Monument Valley Navajo Tribal Park, consisting of 91,696 acres. The park contains a seventeen-mile loop road through the sights. Admission is charged, and there is a visitor center, trading post, and modern hotel completed in 2008. In the Detourists' time, lodging could be acquired at Goulding's Lodge outside of the park. The scenery in Monument Valley, with its 400- to 1,000-foot-high pinnacles and buttes, is so fantastic that it has been the site of countless motion pictures. The first film was shot there in 1925—*The Vanishing American*—based on a Zane Grey novel. Hollywood director John Ford shot ten films in Monument Valley, five of which starred John Wayne. The Navajo trading post has an entire section devoted to John Wayne gifts, with the "largest selection in the Four Corners."

The Four Corners are where the states of Utah, Colorado, New Mexico, and Arizona meet. The spot is about eighty-two miles northeast of Kayenta, Arizona. A plaque marking the location in the middle of a barren desert signaled to the Detourists that they were there. They probably did the same thing that tourists do today—kneel down and spread arms and legs so that one's body is in four states at the same time. Today the Four Corners are in a Navajo Tribal Park and admission is charged. A nice concrete pad is on the ground with a bronze marker delineating the four state boundaries coming together. Navajo arts and craft booths are set up nearby to attract tourist spending. From the Four Corners, the Detourists could choose to go on to Cortez, Colorado, and Mesa Verde National Park, or return to Winslow by way of Canyon de Chelly.

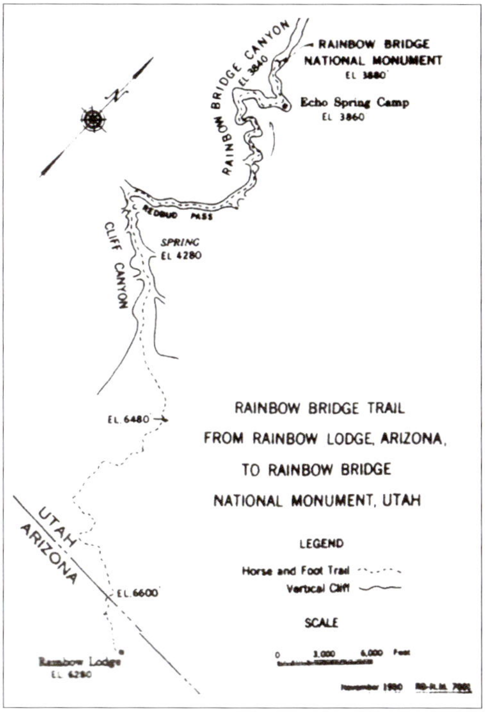

Above left: The horseback/hiking trail from Rainbow Lodge to Rainbow Bridge is shown. The trail is approximately thirteen miles long, requiring an overnight campout. [*National Park Service*]

Above right: George Grant photographed Rainbow Bridge for the National Park Service in 1946.

President Theodore Roosevelt (second from right) and crew at a campsite on the trail to Rainbow Bridge in 1913. [*National Park Service*]

The "mittens" are probably the most famous feature in Monument Valley, which is a Navajo Tribal Park.

The rugged landscape in Monument Valley has been the scene of dozens of motion pictures.

The author demonstrates how to be in four states (New Mexico, Arizona, Utah, and Colorado) at one time at the Four Corners Navajo Tribal Park.

9

A Fred Harvey/Mary Colter Indian Detour to the Grand Canyon

The Indian Detours had their greatest success from 1926 to 1931. By 1931, the Great Depression was having a profound impact upon passenger train travel and touring. Fred Harvey's losses were substantial, and to prevent further losses the Indian Detours were sold to their creator, Hunter Clarkson, on March 16. In 1933, Clarkson's brother Jim joined the firm, and "without Jim's business ability, the Detours would never have survived the Depression years."[1]

The Detours did manage to survive the Depression, but then World War II came along, and train travel was restricted to troop and equipment transport for the war effort. After the war, Americans had a newfound prosperity and were able to purchase their own automobiles and drive on paved roads such as Route 66 across New Mexico. The Indian Detours barely limped along, but they did manage to celebrate their 25th anniversary on May 15, 1951. "In 1951 the employees of the Detours, many of them with the company since its inception, arranged for a Silver Anniversary party … on Tuesday, May 15 … Everyone present was rooting for a rebirth of the tours."[2]

The rebirth miraculously occurred in 1953 when the Detours were revived with the usual one, two, and three-day trips, and Land Cruises from Santa Fe to Canyon de Chelly, Petrified Forest, Painted Desert, the Hopi mesas, and the Grand Canyon. There was a four-day Mesa Verde trip and a three-day Land Cruise to Carlsbad Caverns. That really was the last hurrah though. In 1956, Hunter Clarkson gave the Indian Detours business to his brother, Jim. In 1968, Jim sold the business to Gray Line. Also in 1968, the Fred Harvey Company was sold to Amfac, and the colorful era of Fred Harvey and the Indian Detours came to an end.

In the spirit of that 1953 rebirth, let's take our own imaginary Indian Detour through time from Santa Fe to the Grand Canyon, celebrating all the creations of architect Mary Colter for the Fred Harvey Company along the way. Those creations were all still standing in 1953 except for El Ortiz Hotel in Lamy which had been torn down in 1943. As we have seen, Mary Colter was first hired as a contract employee by Fred Harvey in 1902 to design the interior of the Indian Building at the Alvarado Hotel in Albuquerque. However, our imaginary journey begins in Lamy at El Ortiz Hotel before we board a Harveycar to Santa Fe. Mary Colter provided the interior designs for El Ortiz when it was built in 1910.

> The lounge had the traditional log-beam viga ceiling and a fireplace on which Colter created a geometric Indian design in the brickwork. She furnished the lounge with a heavy carved Mexican table surrounded by brass-studded, straight-backed chairs. The table held a large fern in an Indian pot, and the tile floor was covered with Navajo rugs ... After staying at El Ortiz, Owen Wister, author of *The Virginian*, wrote his compliments to Jacob Stein, the manager. He described El Ortiz as "like a private house of someone who had lavished thought and care upon every nook." Colter must have been pleased, for that was the effect she worked to create.[3]

Our next stop is La Fonda Hotel in Santa Fe, where Colter continued "lavishing thought and care upon every nook" which she designed in every room of the hotel. She also helped Santa Fe architect John Gaw Meem design the expansion of La Fonda from 1926–1929.

After hopping on a Harveycar at La Fonda and heading west across La Bajada Hill, the next stop on our imaginary Detour is the Alvarado Hotel in Albuquerque. Here was Mary Colter's very first assignment for the Harvey Company. In the summer of 1902, Colter received a telegram at her cabin in the woods outside of St. Paul, Minnesota, from Herman Schweizer, telling her:

> to get on a train to New Mexico immediately. Fred Harvey needed her help with a new Indian Museum ... The rooms she created (at the Indian Building) were paradoxical; both entirely faux and deeply, richly authentic, crammed with genuine pieces of native art and crafts set amid pre-weathered, deliberately distressed beams, wooden floors, and brick fireplaces. She took the items that Indians were selling on train platforms

El Ortiz Hotel in Lamy, New Mexico was constructed in 1910 with interior decorations by Mary Colter. Notice the Fred Harvey Newsstand on the left just beyond the sign. [*Photograph by Edward Kemp, Library of Congress, LC-DIG-ds-11580*]

> and put them into context—a context of her own inspiration ... These rooms in Albuquerque felt intimate enough to live in every day—and in fact, appeared as if someone fascinating had been inhabiting them for years. This cross-cultural tableau of fantasy rooms marked the beginning of what we now refer to as "Santa Fe Style."[4]

To see Mary Colter's next creation on our journey we will hop aboard the AT&SF train in Albuquerque and head west to Gallup, departing the train at El Navajo Hotel. Getting off the train we wonder if we are in the right town. The railroad station and hotel look nothing like the Spanish/Pueblo buildings of other Fred Harvey locations. The buildings are square blocks with arches in front. This modernistic architecture seemed to clash with the purpose of the hotel—to pay tribute to the Navajo tribe, hence the name El Navajo Hotel. Another problem was that Mary Colter wanted to decorate the interior walls of the hotel with Navajo sand paintings. Traditionally, the sand painting is created by a Navajo medicine man on the floor of a hogan for a ritualistic purpose. When the blessing is accomplished, the sand painting is destroyed. So why did Colter think she could get a sand painting on the walls of El Navajo?

> Colter had established good relationships over the years with Indian artists and was consequently in a position to achieve a remarkable "first" in El Navajo: she was allowed to use Indian sand paintings as a decorative motif throughout the hotel.[5]

The exterior of the Alvarado Hotel in Albuquerque was photographed in 1969 by the Historic American Buildings Survey, just prior to its demolition in 1970. [*Library of Congress, HABS NM-123-15*]

Indians selling their wares to tourists in front of Fred Harvey's Indian Building at the Alvarado Hotel, c. 1910. [*Library of Congress, LC-USZ62-97656*]

"Photostint" color postcards were converted from black-and-white photographs (such as the previous photograph) by a process developed in 1906 and used by Fred Harvey for promotional purposes.

The interior of the Indian Building decorated by Mary Colter is illustrated in this Fred Harvey photostint postcard.

The sand paintings were copied meticulously onto the interior walls of the hotel, and the hotel opened on May 26, 1923.

From El Navajo we'll climb back aboard a Harveycar and head west into Arizona. Our first stop is at the Painted Desert Inn in what is now Petrified Forest National Park. The inn was remodeled in 1938 in Pueblo style by the Civilian Conservation Corps with six small guest rooms, a lunchroom, dining room, and gift shop. Fred Harvey took over concessions there in 1947 and asked Mary Colter to design the interior of the building. Colter called upon her old acquaintance, Fred Kabotie, to paint murals of Hopi legends on the walls, and skylights were painted with Hopi pottery designs. Today, the building is a visitor center/museum for the National Park.

Heading west on our Fred Harvey/Mary Colter Detour, the next stop is La Posada Hotel in Winslow, Arizona. La Posada was completed in 1930, and Indian Detours then departed from there rather than from Gallup. Mary Colter completely dreamed up this building.

> When La Posada opened in May 1930, it was clear that Colter had conjured her most eccentric structure ever. It was a faux-Spanish hacienda purposely designed to have a kind of architectural multiple personality disorder … She invented an elaborate backstory to explain why the eclectic building appeared to have been designed by unrelated architects over many decades.[6]

Colter's Spanish hacienda interior was decorated with crude wooden furniture to replicate the feeling of an ancient hacienda. However, it also had beautiful decorations

Above: El Navajo Hotel in Gallup, New Mexico, opened in 1923. It was a break from the usual pueblo-style buildings. The hotel was on the right and the AT&SF station was on the left with the arched entryway.

Right: El Navajo Hotel was demolished in 1957, but the station remains today, as seen with the arched entryway to the right.

Fred Harvey took over concessions at the Painted Desert Inn (viewed here in 2023) from 1947 to 1963, and Mary Colter designed the interior with Fred Kabotie paintings on the walls.

Guests sit at the Fred Harvey lunch counter at Painted Desert Inn c. 1950. Notice the sign for "Lily Ice Cream" and the design of the chairs, both seen in the restored lunchroom in the next photograph. [*National Park Service*]

Restoration of the Fred Harvey lunchroom and dining room occurred from 2004–2006.

A mural painted by Fred Kabotie above Fred Harvey dining booths at Painted Desert Inn.

from Europe which a Spanish family would have brought with them to the New World. This fantasy hotel was a welcome relief from the hot Arizona sun and provided a great departure place for Harveycar tours of the Hopi reservation.

We come to the end of our journey at the Grand Canyon where Mary Colter created many buildings over the years. Travel to the Grand Canyon was primitive before 1901 as stagecoaches brought intrepid visitors along the hot dusty roads. In 1901, the Atchison, Topeka, and Santa Fe Railway completed a sixty-mile spur line from Williams, Arizona, to the south rim of the Grand Canyon, opening the floodgates of tourist travel to the Canyon.

> For the following half century, Santa Fe Railroad officials built nearly all of the (Grand Canyon) village's hotels, restaurants, curio shops, rest stops, lookouts, and public utilities. During 1901–19 they and their partner, the Fred Harvey Company, determined what would be built and where, reserving the rim for tourist amenities.[7]

And the Fred Harvey Company decided that Mary Colter should design most of those amenities. While the El Tovar Hotel was being built in 1904, Colter was busy with construction of Hopi House across from it. Both buildings opened in January 1905. "Since the Hopis had inhabited the Grand Canyon area for centuries, Colter designed a building in the style of a Hopi dwelling, after those at Oraibi, Arizona. The building was to house the main salesrooms for Fred Harvey Indian arts."[8] The building was not only for art sales, as Hopi Indians were brought in to demonstrate various arts such

Mary Colter designed La Posada Hotel in Winslow, Arizona, as a Spanish hacienda supposedly developed in segments over periods of time.

as weaving and pottery. Hopis would also provide dances for the tourists outside the building in the evening. The building was made of local stone and logs and was terraced with ladders reaching to the upper levels. Some of the Hopis who worked in the building lived on the upper floors.

With the completion of El Tovar, a road was constructed west along the rim for seven miles. Tourist facilities were needed along the road and Colter designed two in 1914. Heading west, the first was known as the Lookout or Lookout Studio. It was a stone building blending in with the edge of the canyon.

> It was designed as a place from which people could view and photograph the canyon. On the porch were high-powered telescopes providing visitors with a closer view of the gorge. Inside, the Lookout was a neat, comfortable, rustic studio of stone and log timbers. It contained a fireplace alcove and an art room where postcards, photographs, and paintings were for sale.[9]

At the end of the seven-mile road was Hermit's Rest. Here we can depart from our Harveycar and have refreshments in this primitive building. "Hermit's Rest was designed by Colter to look like a dwelling constructed by an untrained mountain man using the natural timber and boulders of the area."[10]

As visitation to the Grand Canyon increased after World War I, Fred Harvey began mule trips for visitors to the bottom of the Canyon. It was eight miles down on the Kaibab Trail. A facility was needed at the bottom, and Mary Colter was called upon to design Phantom Ranch. In 1921, a suspension bridge was built across the Colorado River, and in 1922 Phantom Ranch was completed. The cabins were built of local stone, and the Ranch had a large dining hall and a recreation hall. As many as seventy-five visitors could be accommodated at the ranch.

The illustration shows the hodgepodge of buildings and architectural styles which have been developed at the Grand Canyon since 1905 when El Tovar Hotel and Hopi House opened. In the village, Mary Colter designed Hopi House, Bright Angel Lodge, and Lookout Studio.

Hopi House, designed by Mary Colter, opened in 1905, based on Hopi dwellings she had seen at Oraibi on Third Mesa. [*National Park Service*]

Hopi House in 2018 appears much the same as in the previous photograph. Mary Colter's designs have stood the test of time. [*Photograph by Carol Highsmith, Library of Congress, LC-DIG-highsm-54361*]

The interior of Hopi House today displays a wide range of Indian arts and crafts for sale, just as it did in Fred Harvey days.

Albert Einstein visited the Grand Canyon in 1931 and posed with an Indian headdress and pipe in front of Hopi House. Others in the photograph are from left: E. B. Duffy (AT&SF passenger agent), Herman Schweizer (Fred Harvey Indian arts buyer), Leo Humequaftewa, Einstein, Mrs. Einstein, Lucy Timeche, unidentified child, Chester Dennis, Porter Timeche (with drum). [*National Park Service*]

Above left: Mary Colter perched Lookout Studio on the edge of the Grand Canyon, using local stone to blend in with the edge. Telescopes were placed in the Studio for viewing the Canyon.

Above right: Lookout Studio today still offers visitors a view of the Grand Canyon through telescopes.

El Tovar Hotel sits on the edge of the Grand Canyon as viewed from Lookout Studio.

A 1915 promotional brochure for the AT&SF showed tourists in a coach headed out on the Hermit Rim Road from El Tovar Hotel. At the end of the road, they would visit Hermits Rest, designed by Mary Colter.

A Harveycoach loads tourists aboard at El Tovar in the 1920s for a drive on the Hermit Rim Drive. Shuttle buses drive the same road today, as passenger cars are not allowed on the road during the busy summer months. [*National Park Service*]

Mary Colter designed Hermits Rest as a primitive place where a Grand Canyon hermit or mountain man might have lived. This is the entrance.

Above left: Again using local stone and timber, Mary Colter designed Hermits Rest to look like a cave dwelling on the rim of the Grand Canyon.

Above right: A large fireplace dominates the interior of Hermits Rest, and the cozy room provided a place to sell Fred Harvey souvenirs, postcards, and snacks.

Mary Colter designed the facilities at Phantom Ranch which opened in 1922 at the bottom of the Grand Canyon. Facilities included the cabins seen here, a dining hall, and a recreation hall. [*National Park Service*]

A swimming pool was added at Phantom Ranch for the guests' comfort. Plagued by drainage and water problems, the pool was covered in 1972. [*National Park Service*]

From El Tovar east the road leads twenty-five miles along the Canyon rim to Desert View.

> In 1928 the National Park Service, Fred Harvey Company, and Santa Fe Railroad began to develop Desert View as the eastern gateway to Grand Canyon's South Rim. Their centerpiece was the "Indian Watchtower," a steel-framed structure whose inspiration was the prehistoric stone towers built eight hundred years ago in the Four Corners region.[11]

Mary Colter had visited the Ancestral Pueblo ruins at Mesa Verde and Hovenweep, Colorado, and she had seen the round stone towers which inspired her vision for the Desert View Watchtower. The tower was seventy feet high and thirty feet wide. The exterior of the circular steel frame was covered by local stone. Colter had Hopi artist, Fred Kabotie, paint the interior walls with symbols and legends. The ground floor was a large round observation room with glass windows overlooking the Grand Canyon. Stairs ascended to the next floor which was the Hopi Room with walls painted with the Snake Legend, the basis for the Hopi Snake Dance. Completed in 1932, the Watchtower still stands, one of Mary Colter's most notable creations.

Heading back west from the Watchtower in our Harveycar, we stop for the night at the Bright Angel Lodge, a Mary Colter design completed in 1935.

> Since Bright Angel Lodge was to be more moderately priced than El Tovar, Colter designed a pioneer-style building in natural wood tones like the older hotel. ... The Bright Angel Lodge facilities consisted not only of a new lodge with shops and restaurants, but also of a little village of individual cabins.[12]

After a relaxing night at Bright Angel Lodge, we walk past El Tovar Hotel and down to the train station, where our AT&SF train will take us back to Williams for our connection with the Super Chief, heading west to Los Angeles. We can hardly believe all we have seen of Mary Colter's work across New Mexico and Arizona. She was truly inspired by the Native people, the historic ruins, and the grand landscape. "The fact that all of Colter's Grand Canyon buildings still stand and serve historic functions, despite the changing cultural landscape of the past century, is testament to the high esteem others have held for her work."[13] Mary Colter retired to a home in Santa Fe and passed away there on January 8, 1958. Thus concludes our special Indian Detour of 1953 inspired by the works of the Fred Harvey Company's most famous architect—Mary Elizabeth Jane Colter.

Above left: A Harveycar driver helps Mary Colter examine a tower ruin at Hovenweep National Monument in 1931. This tower and the ones at Mesa Verde provided the inspiration for Colter's Desert View Watchtower at the Grand Canyon. [*National Park Service*]

Above right: AT&SF bridge designers provided the interior steel structural design for Mary Colter's Desert View Watchtower. Local stone then was used to cover the circular steel frame. The tower was completed in 1932. [*National Park Service*]

Above left: The completed Watchtower is simply astounding.

Above right: Harveycoaches line up at the Watchtower to take tourists back west to El Tovar Hotel in the 1930s. [*National Park Service*]

Above left: Mary Colter enlisted her Hopi friend, Fred Kabotie, to paint murals on the inside walls of the Desert View Watchtower.

Above right: A circular staircase inside the Watchtower leads visitors up four stories to the top. Illustrations by Fred Kabotie and others adorn all the walls.

Bright Angel Lodge, designed by Mary Colter in a Western rustic style, offered a cheaper alternative for overnight guests than the more formal El Tovar Hotel. Bright Angel consists of the lodge, restaurants, and cabins.

Endnotes

Introduction

1. Cobb, I. S., Roughing It De Luxe (New York: George H. Duran Company, 1914), p. 17 & 27.
2. Taggett, S. C. and Schwarz, T., Paintbrushes and Pistols: How the Taos Artists Sold the West (Santa Fe, NM: John Muir Publications, 1990), p. 47.
3. Fried, S., Appetite for America: Fred Harvey and the Business of Civilizing the Wild West—One Meal at a Time (New York: Bantam Books, 2010), p. 43.
4. Howard, K. and Pardue, D., Over the Edge: Fred Harvey at the Grand Canyon and in the Great Southwest (Tucson, AZ: Rio Nuevo Publishers, 2016), p. 1.
5. Ibid., p. 5.
6. Fried, op.cit., p. xviii.
7. Manchester, A. D., Trails Begin Where Rails End: Early-day Motoring Adventures in the West and Southwest (Glendale, CA: Trans-Anglo Books, 1987), p. 145.

Chapter 1

1. Howard, K., and Pardue, D., *Inventing the Southwest: The Fred Harvey Company and Native American Art* (Flagstaff, AZ: Northland Publishing Company, 1998), p. 123.
2. *Ibid.*
3. Anderson, M. F., *Along the Rim: A Guide to Grand Canyon's South Rim from Hermits Rest to Desert View* (Grand Canyon, AZ: Grand Canyon Association, 2001), p. 53.
4. Fried, *Appetite for America.*, p. 282.
5. Fried, S., *La Fonda Then and Now* (Santa Fe, NM: La Fonda Holdings, LLC, 2016) p. 14.
6. Fried, *Appetite for America*, p. 283.
7. Thomas, D. H., *The Southwestern Indian Detours* (Phoenix, AZ: Hunter Publishing Co., 1978) p. 61.
8. *Ibid.*
9. *Ibid.*, p. 63.
10. *Ibid.*, p. 96.
11. *Ibid.*, p. 75.
12. Fried, *Appetite for America*, p. 284.
13. Thomas, *op.cit.*, p. 88.
14. Manchester, *Trails Begin Where Rails End*, p. 127.
15. Thomas, *op.cit.*, pp. 98-99.

16. *Ibid.*, p. 113.
17. Howard, *Over the Edge*, pp. 102-104.
18. Fried, *La Fonda Then and Now*, p. 14.
19. *Ibid.*, p. 9.

Chapter 2

1. Fried, *Appetite for America*, p. 288.
2. Crampton, C. G., *The Zunis of Cibola* (Salt Lake City, UT: University of Utah Press, 1979), p. 120.
3. Weber, D. J. and deBuys, W., *First Impressions: A Reader's Journey to Iconic Places of the American Southwest* (New Haven, CT: Yale University Press, 2017), p. 241.
4. Leavitt, V. C., *Eanger Irving Couse: Image Maker for America* (Albuquerque, NM: The Albuquerque Museum, 2006) p. 36.
5. McLuhan, T. C., *Dream Tracks: The Railroad and the American Indian 1890 – 1930* (New York: Harry N. Abrams, Inc., Publishers, 1984), p. 18.
6. *Ibid.,* p. 30.
7. *Ibid.,* pp. 18-19.
8. Fried, *Appetite for America*, p. 183.
9. Howard, *Inventing the Southwest*, p. 41.
10. Fried, *La Fonda Then and Now*, p. 12.
11. Howard, *Over the Edge*, p. 57.
12. Howard, *Inventing the Southwest*, p. 44.
13. *Ibid.*, p. 128
14. *Ibid.*, p. 131.
15. *Ibid.*, p. 89.
16. Howard, *Over the Edge*, p. 8.
17. Dye, V., *All Aboard for Santa Fe: Railway Promotion of the Southwest, 1890s to 1930s* (Albuquerque, NM: University of New Mexico Press, 2006), p. 136, note 68.
18. *Ibid.*, p. 52.
19. Howard, *Inventing the Southwest*, pp. 133-134.

Chapter 3

1. Thomas, *The Southwestern Indian Detours*, p. 45.
2. *Ibid.*, pp. 45-46.
3. *Ibid.*, p. 67.
4. Poling-Kempes, L., *The Harvey Girls: Women Who Opened the West* (New York: Paragon House, 1989), p. 150.
5. National Park Service, *Pecos National Historical Park Brochure.*
6. Thomas, *op.cit.*, p. 68.
7. Hayes, A. and Blom, J., *Southwestern Pottery Anasazi to Zuni* (Flagstaff, AZ: Northland Publishing, 1996), p. 154.
8. *Ibid.*
9. Fergusson, E., *Dancing Gods: Indian Ceremonials of New Mexico and Arizona* (Albuquerque, NM: University of New Mexico Press, 1966 edition), p. 54.
10. *Ibid.*, p. 42.
11. Simmons, M. (foreword), *The WPA Guide to 1930s New Mexico* (Tucson, AZ: University of Arizona Press, 1989), p. 353.
12. Gibson, D. *Pueblos of the Rio Grande: A Visitor's Guide* (Tucson, AZ: Rio Nuevo Publishers, 2001), p. 70.

13. Fergusson, *op.cit.*, p. 56.
14. Hayes, *op.cit.*, p. 130.
15. Fergusson, *op.cit.*, pp. 56-57.
16. Gibson, *op.cit.*, p. 77.
17. Mays, B. *Indian Villages of the Southwest: A Practical Guide to the Pueblo Indian Villages of New Mexico and Arizona* (San Francisco, CA: Chronicle Books, 1985), p. 28.

Chapter 4

1. Santa Fe New Mexican, March 7, 1933, quoted in Thomas, *The Southwestern Indian Detours*, pp. 272-273.
2. Gibson, *Pueblos of the Rio Grande*, p. 59.
3. Butler, M., *Tracking the Chili Line Railroad to Santa Fe* (Charleston, SC: Fonthill Media and Arcadia Publishing, 2020), p. 102.
4. Schwartz, D. W., *Bandelier National Monument: Geology, History, Prehistory* (Santa Fe, NM: School of American Research, 1980), Introduction.
5. Greene, E. J. *Bandelier National Monument: Geology, History, Prehistory* (Santa Fe, NM: School of American Research, 1980), p. 24.
6. Thomas, *The Southwestern Indian Detours*, p. 277.
7. Melzer, R., *Coming of Age in the Great Depression: The Civilian Conservation Corps Experience in New Mexico*, 1933-1942 (Las Cruces, NM: Yucca Tree Press, 2000), p. 67.
8. Butler, M., *Images of America: High Road to Taos* (Charleston, SC: Arcadia Publishing, 2016), p. 11.
9. *Ibid.*, p. 122.
10. Butler, M., *Taos: A Pictorial Guide for Travelers* (Santa Fe, NM: Sunstone Press, 2019), p. 10.

Chapter 5

1. Thomas, *The Southwestern Indian Detours*, pp., 162-163.
2. *Ibid.*, p. 165.
3. National Park Service, *Chaco Culture National Historical Park Brochure*.
4. McBrinn, M. (editor), *Oblique Views: Aerial Photography and Southwest Archaeology* (Santa Fe, NM: Museum of New Mexico Press, 2015), p. 73.
5. National Park Service, *op.cit.*, *Chaco Culture*
6. Noble, D. G., *Ancient Ruins of the Southwest: An Archaeological Guide* (Flagstaff, AZ: Northland Press, 2000), p. 57.
7. Atchison, Topeka and Santa Fe Railway, *1930 Detours Brochure*.
8. *Ibid.*
9. Melzer, R., *Images of America: Fred Harvey Houses of the Southwest* (Charleston, SC: Arcadia Publishing, 2008), p. 64.
10. Greene, E. J. *Carlsbad Caverns: The Story Behind the Scenery* (Las Vegas, NV: KC Publications, 2007), p 33.
11. Thomas, *op.cit.*, p. 172.
12. *Ibid.*, p. 174
13. *Ibid.*, p. 215

Chapter 6

1. Thomas, *The Southwestern Indian Detours*, p. 133.
2. *Ibid.*, p. 136.
3. Gibson, *Pueblos of the Rio Grande*, p. 36.

4. Thomas, *op.cit.*, p. 134.
5. Gibson, *op.cit.*, p. 19.
6. *Ibid.*, p. 38.
7. Thomas, *op.cit.*, p. 292.

CHAPTER 7

1. Julyan, R. *The Place Names of New Mexico* (Albuquerque, NM: University of New Mexico Press, 1998), p. 144.
2. Simmons, *WPA Guide to 1930s New Mexico*, p. 324.
3. Gibson, *Pueblos of the Rio Grande*, p. 90.
4. www.icecaves.com
5. Brugge, D. M. and Wilson, R., *Administrative History Canyon de Chelly National Monument Arizona* (National Park Service, 1976), not paginated.
6. *Ibid.*
7. Supplee, C. and Anderson, D., *Canyon de Chelly: The Story Behind the Scenery* (Las Vegas, NV: KC Publications, 1990), p. 12.
8. Thomas, *The Southwestern Indian Detours*, p. 226.
9. National Park Service, *Canyon de Chelly National Monument Brochure.*

CHAPTER 8

1. Ash, S., *Petrified Forest: The Story Behind the Scenery* (Las Vegas, NV: KC Publications, 1986), p. 12.
2. *Ibid.*, pp. 12-14.
3. Kosik, F., *Native Roads: The Complete Motoring Guide to the Navajo and Hopi Nations* (Tucson, AZ: Rio Nuevo Publishers, 2013), p. 128.
4. Thomas, *The Southwestern Indian Detours*, p. 230.
5. *Ibid.*, p. 252.
6. Fergusson, *Dancing Gods*, p. 148.
7. Kosik, *op.cit.*, p. 18.
8. *Ibid.*
9. *Ibid.*, p. 20.
10. National Park Service, *Rainbow Bridge National Monument Brochure.*

CHAPTER 9

1. Thomas, *The Southwestern Indian Detours*, pp. 306-307.
2. *Ibid.*, p. 319.
3. Grattan, V. L., *Mary Colter Builder Upon the Red Earth* (Grand Canyon, AZ: Grand Canyon Conservancy, 2019) pp. 22-25.
4. Fried, *Appetite for America*, pp. 185-186.
5. Grattan, *op.cit.*, p. 42.
6. Fried, *op.cit.*, pp. 322-323.
7. Anderson, *Along the Rim*, pp. 11-13.
8. Grattan, *op.cit.*, p. 14.
9. *Ibid.*, p. 26.
10. *Ibid.*
11. Anderson, *op.cit.*, p. 67.
12. Grattan, *op.cit.*, pp. 82-84.
13. Anderson, *op.cit.*, p. 55.

Bibliography

Anderson, M. F., *Along the Rim: A Guide to Grand Canyon's South Rim from Hermits Rest to Desert View* (Grand Canyon, AZ: Grand Canyon Association, 2001)

Ash, S., *Petrified Forest: The Story Behind the Scenery* (Las Vegas, NV: KC Publications, 1986)

Atchison, Topeka and Santa Fe Railway, *1930 Detours Brochure*

Butler, M., *Images of America: High Road to Taos* (Charleston, SC: Arcadia Publishing, 2016)

Butler, M., *Taos: A Pictorial Guide for Travelers* (Santa Fe, NM: Sunstone Press, 2019)

Butler, M., *Tracking the Chili Line Railroad to Santa Fe* (Charleston, SC: Fonthill Media and Arcadia Publishing, 2020)

Brugge, D.M. and Wilson, R., *Administrative History Canyon de Chelly National Monument Arizona* (National Park Service, 1976)

Cash, M. R. *Built of Earth and Song: Churches of Northern New Mexico* (Santa Fe, NM: Red Crane Books, 1993)

Cobb, I. S., *Roughing It De Luxe* (New York: George H. Duran Company, 1914)

Crampton, C. G., *The Zunis of Cibola* (Salt Lake City, UT: University of Utah Press, 1979)

Dye, V., *All Aboard for Santa Fe: Railway Promotion of the Southwest, 1890s to 1930s* (Albuquerque, NM: University of New Mexico Press, 2006)

Fergusson, E., *Dancing Gods: Indian Ceremonials of New Mexico and Arizona* (Albuquerque, NM: University of New Mexico Press, 1966 edition)

Fried, S. *Appetite for America: Fred Harvey and the Business of Civilizing the Wild West—One Meal at a Time* (New York: Bantam Books, 2010)

Fried, S. *La Fonda Then and Now* (Santa Fe, NM: La Fonda Holdings, LLC, 2016)

Gibson, D., *Pueblos of the Rio Grande: A visitor's Guide* (Tucson, AZ: Rio Nuevo Publishers, 2001)

Grattan, V. L., *Mary Colter Builder Upon the Red Earth* (Grand Canyon, AZ: Grand Canyon Conservancy, 2019)

Greene, E. J. *Bandelier National Monument: Geology, History, Prehistory* (Santa Fe, NM: School of American Research, 1980)

Greene, E. J. *Carlsbad Caverns: The Story Behind the Scenery* (Las Vegas, NV: KC Publications, 2007)

Hayes, A. and Blom, J. *Southwestern Pottery Anasazi to Zuni* (Flagstaff, AZ: Northland Publishing, 1996)

Howard, K. and Pardue, D., *Inventing the Southwest: The Fred Harvey Company and Native American Art* (Flagstaff, AZ: Northland Publishing Company, 1998)

Howard, K. and Pardue, D., *Over the Edge: Fred Harvey at the Grand Canyon and in the Great Southwest* (Tucson, AZ: Rio Nuevo Publishers, 2016)

Icecaves.com

Julyan, R., *The Place Names of New Mexico* (Albuquerque, NM: University of New Mexico Press, 1998)

Kemp, E., *Santa Fe Harveycars Taos Cruise* (Kansas City, MO: Fred Harvey Company, c. 1928)

Kosik, F., *Native Roads: The Complete Motoring Guide to the Navajo and Hopi Nations* (Tucson, AZ: Rio Nuevo Publishers, 2013)

Leavitt, V. C., *Eanger Irving Couse: Image Maker for America* (Albuquerque, NM: The Albuquerque Museum, 2006)

Manchester, A. D., *Trails Begin Where Rails End: Early-day Motoring Adventures in the West and Southwest* (Glendale, CA: Trans-Anglo Books, 1987)

Mays, B., *Indian Villages of the Southwest: A Practical Guide to the Pueblo Indian Villages of New Mexico and Arizona* (San Francisco, CA: Chronicle Books, 1985)

McBrinn, M., *Oblique Views: Aerial Photography and Southwest Archaeology* (Santa Fe, NM: Museum of New Mexico Press, 2015)

McLuhan, T. C., *Dream Tracks: The Railroad and the American Indian 1890 – 1930* (New York: Harry N. Abrams, Inc., Publishers, 1984)

Melzer, R., *Coming of Age in the Great Depression: The Civilian Conservation Corps Experience in New Mexico, 1933 – 1942* (Las Cruces, NM: Yucca Tree Press, 2000)

Melzer, R., *Images of America: Fred Harvey Houses of the Southwest* (Charleston, SC: Arcadia Publishing, 2008)

National Park Service, *Canyon de Chelly National Monument Brochure*

National Park Service, *Chaco Culture National Historical Park Brochure*

National Park Service, *Pecos National Historical Park Brochure*

National Park Service, *Rainbow Bridge National Monument Brochure*

Noble, D. G., *Ancient Ruins of the Southwest: An Archaeological Guide* (Flagstaff, AZ: Northland Press, 2000)

Poling-Kempes, L., *The Harvey Girls: Women Who Opened the West* (New York: Paragon House, 1989)

Santa Fe New Mexican, March 7, 1933, in Thomas, D.H., *The Southwestern Indian Detours* (Phoenix, AZ: Hunter Publishing Co., 1978)

Schwarz, D. W., *Bandelier National Monument: Geology, History, Prehistory* (Santa Fe, NM: School of American Research, 1980)

Simmons, M., *The WPA Guide to 1930s New Mexico* (Tucson, AZ: University of Arizona Press, 1989)

Supplee, C. and Anderson, D., *Canyon de Chelly: The Story Behind the Scenery* (Las Vegas, NV: KC Publications, 1990)

Taggett, S. C. and Schwarz, T., *Paintbrushes and Pistols: How the Taos Artists Sold the West* (Santa Fe, NM: John Muir Publications, 1990)

Thomas, D. H., *The Southwestern Indian Detours* (Phoenix, AZ: Hunter Publishing Co., 1978)

Weber, D. J. and deBuys, W., *First Impressions: A Reader's Journey to Iconic Places of the American Southwest* (New Haven, CT: Yale University Press, 2017)